GRADES
3-4

...the Super Source®
Tangrams

Cuisenaire Company of America, Inc.
White Plains, NY

Cuisenaire extends its warmest thanks to the many teachers and students across the country who helped ensure the success of the Super Source® series by participating in the outlining, writing, and field testing of the materials.

Project Director: Judith Adams
Managing Editor: Doris Hirschhorn
Editorial Team: Patricia Kijak Anderson, Linda Dodge, John Nelson, Deborah J. Slade, Harriet Slonim
Field Test Coordinator: Laurie Verdeschi

Design Manager: Phyllis Aycock
Text Design: Amy Berger, Tracey Munz
Line Art and Production: Joan Lee, Fiona Santoianni
Cover Design: Michael Muldoon
Illustrations: Rebecca Thornburgh

...the Super Source®
Table of Contents

Using the Super Source™

The Super Source™ is a series of books, each of which contains a collection of activities to use with a specific math manipulative. Driving **the Super Source**™ is Cuisenaire's conviction that children construct their own understandings through rich, hands-on mathematical experiences. Although the activities in each book are written for a specific grade range, they all connect to the core of mathematics learning that is important to every K-6 child. Thus, the material in many activities can easily be refocused for children at other grade levels. Because the activities are not arranged sequentially, children can work on any activity at any time.

The lessons in **the Super Source**™ all follow a basic structure consistent with the vision of mathematics teaching described in the *Curriculum and Evaluation Standards for School Mathematics* published by the National Council of Teachers of Mathematics.

All of the activities in this series involve Problem Solving, Communication, Reasoning, and Mathematical Connections—the first four NCTM Standards. Each activity also focuses on one or more of the following curriculum strands: Number, Geometry, Measurement, Patterns/Functions, Probability/Statistics, Logic.

HOW LESSONS ARE ORGANIZED

At the beginning of each lesson, you will find, to the right of the title, both the major curriculum strands to which the lesson relates and the particular topics that children will work with. Each lesson has three main sections. The first, GETTING READY, offers an *Overview*, which states what children will be doing, and why, and provides a list of "What You'll Need." Specific numbers of Tangram pieces or entire sets are suggested on this list but can be adjusted as the needs of your specific situation dictate. Before the activity, Tangram pieces or sets can be counted out and placed in containers or self-sealing plastic bags for easy distribution. Blackline masters that are provided for your convenience at the back of the book are referenced on this materials list. Paper, pencils, scissors, tape, and materials for making charts, which may be necessary in some activities, are not.

Although overhead Tangram pieces and overhead Tangram recording paper are always listed in "What You'll Need" as optional, these materials are highly effective when you want children to see a demonstration using Tangrams. As you move the pieces on the screen, children can work with the same materials at their seats. Children can also use the overhead to present their work to other members of their group or to the class.

The second section, THE ACTIVITY, first presents a possible scenario for *Introducing* the children to the activity. The aim of this brief introduction is to help you give children the tools they will need to investigate independently. However, care has been taken to avoid undercutting the activity itself. Since these investigations are designed to enable children to increase their own mathematical power, the idea is to set the stage but not steal the show! The heart of the lesson, *On Their Own*, is found in a box at the top of the second page of each lesson. Here, rich problems stimulate many different problem-solving approaches and lead to a variety of solutions. These hands-on explorations have the potential for bringing children to new mathematical ideas and deepening skills.

On Their Own is intended as a stand-alone activity for children to explore with a partner or in a small group. Be sure to make the needed directions clearly visible. You may want to write them on the chalkboard or on an overhead or present them either on reusable cards or paper. For children who may have difficulty reading the directions, you can read them aloud or make sure that at least one "reader" is in each group.

The last part of this second section, *The Bigger Picture*, gives suggestions for how children can share their work and their thinking and make mathematical connections. Class charts and children's recorded work provide a springboard for discussion. Under "Thinking and Sharing," there are several prompts that you can use to promote discussion. Children will not be able to respond to these prompts with one-word answers. Instead, the prompts encourage children to describe what they notice, tell how they found their results, and give the reasoning behind their answers. Thus children learn to verify their own results rather than relying on the teacher to determine if an answer is "right" or "wrong." Though the class discussion might immediately follow the investigation, it is important not to cut the activity short by having a class discussion too soon.

The Bigger Picture often includes a suggestion for a "Writing" (or drawing) assignment. This is meant to help children process what they have just been doing. You might want to use these ideas as a focus for daily or weekly entries in a math journal that each child keeps.

4. After I made a 7 piece rectangle. I just moved the biggest triangle to the other end of the rectangle to make a paralelagram.

From: *Polygon Parade*

I made a shape with 7 sides and 4 different shapes with 6 sides. I couldn't make one trapazoid.

From: *One Change at a Time*

The Bigger Picture always ends with ideas for "Extending the Activity." Extensions take the essence of the main activity and either alter or extend its parameters. These activities are well used with a class that becomes deeply involved in the primary activity or for children who finish before the others. In any case, it is probably a good idea to expose the entire class to the possibility of, and the results from, such extensions.

The third and final section of the lesson is TEACHER TALK. Here, in *Where's the Mathematics?*, you can gain insight into the underlying mathematics of the activity and discover some of the strategies children are apt to use as they work. Solutions are also given—when such are necessary and/or helpful. Because *Where's the Mathematics?* provides a view of what may happen in the lesson as well as the underlying mathematical potential that may grow out of it, this may be the section that you want to read before presenting the activity to children.

USING THE ACTIVITIES

The Super Source™ has been designed to fit into the variety of classroom environments in which it will be used. These range from a completely manipulative-based classroom to one in which manipulatives are just beginning to play a part. You may choose to use some activities in *the Super Source*™ in the way set forth in each lesson (introducing an activity to the whole class, then breaking the class up into groups that all work on the same task, and so forth). You will then be able to circulate among the groups as they work to observe and perhaps comment on each child's work. This approach requires a full classroom set of materials but allows you to concentrate on the variety of ways that children respond to a given activity.

Alternatively, you may wish to make two or three related activities available to different groups of children at the same time. You may even wish to use different manipulatives to explore the same mathematical concept. (Pattern Blocks and Geoboards, for example, can be used to teach some of the same geometric principles as Tangrams.) This approach does not require full classroom sets of a particular manipulative. It also permits greater adaptation of materials to individual children's needs and/or preferences.

If children are comfortable working independently, you might want to set up a "menu"— that is, set out a number of related activities from which children can choose. Children should be encouraged to write about their experiences with these independent activities.

However you choose to use *the Super Source*™ activities, it would be wise to allow time for several groups or the entire class to share their experiences. The dynamics of this type of interaction, where children share not only solutions and strategies but also feelings and intuitions, is the basis of continued mathematical growth. It allows children who are beginning to form a mathematical structure to clarify it and those who have mastered just isolated concepts to begin to see how these concepts might fit together.

Again, both the individual teaching style and combined learning styles of the children should dictate the specific method of utilizing *the Super Source*™ lessons. At first sight, some activities may appear too difficult for some of your children, and you may find yourself tempted to actually "teach" by modeling exactly how an activity can lead to a particular learning outcome. If you do this, you rob children of the chance to try the activity in whatever way they can. As long as children have a way to begin an investigation, give them time and opportunity to see it through. Instead of making assumptions about what children will or won't do, watch and listen. The excitement and challenge of the activity—as well as the chance to work cooperatively—may bring out abilities in children that will surprise you.

If you are convinced, however, that an activity does not suit your students, adjust it, by all means. You may want to change the language, either by simplifying it or by referring to specific vocabulary that you and your children already use and are comfortable with. On the other hand, if you suspect that an activity isn't challenging enough, you may want to read through the activity extensions for a variation that you can give children instead.

RECORDING

Although the direct process of working with Tangrams is a valuable one, it is afterward, when children look at, compare, share, and think about their constructions, that an activity yields its greatest rewards. However, because it is not always possible to leave Tangram constructions intact, children need an effective way to record their work and need to be encouraged to find ways to transfer their Tangram shapes. To this end, at the back of this book, Tangram paper is provided for reproduction, as are outlines of the Tangram pieces.

It is important that children use a method of recording that they feel comfortable with. Frustration in recording their shapes can leave children feeling that the actual activity was either too difficult or just not fun! Thus, recording methods that are appropriate for a specific class or for specific children might be suggested. For example, children might choose to trace each Tangram piece in their shape onto Tangram paper or onto plain paper, to cut out, color, and tape or paste down paper Tangram pieces, or to use a Tangram template to reproduce the pieces that make up their shapes. You can buy a TANplate, which includes all of the Tangram pieces, or you can make homemade templates by carefully cutting out each shape from a plastic coffee-can lid.

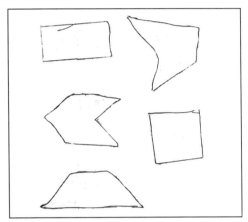

From: *It Can Be Arranged*

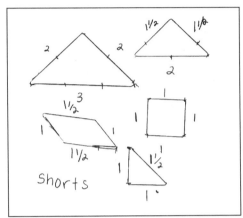

From: *The Long and Short of It*

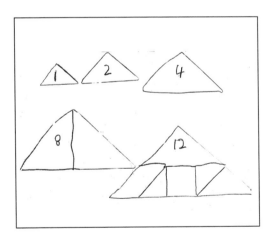

From: *Triangle Mania*

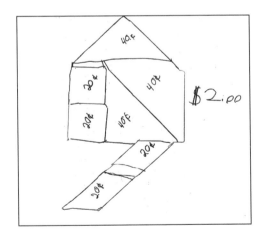

From: *Shopping for Shapes*

Another interesting way to "freeze" a Tangram shape is to create it using a software piece, such as *Journey with Tangrams* or *Shape Up!*, and then get a printout. Children can use a classroom or resource room computer if it is available or, where possible, extend the activity into a home assignment by utilizing their home computers. Since both children and adults enjoy Tangram puzzles, Tangrams, whether "in hand" or "on screen," can prove very helpful in making the home-school connection.

For many Tangram activities, recording involves copying the placement of the Tangram pieces. Yet, since there is a natural progression from thinking with manipulatives to a verbal description of what was done to a written record of it, as children work through the Tangram activities they should also be encouraged to record their thinking processes. Writing, drawing, and making charts and tables are also ways to record. By creating a table of data gathered in the course of their investigations, children are able to draw conclusions and look for patterns. When children write or draw, either in their group or later by themselves, they are clarifying their understanding of their recent mathematical experience.

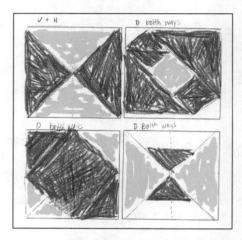

From: *Design It with Symmetry*

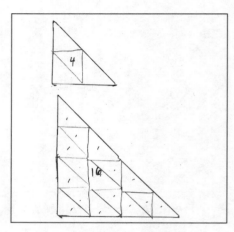

From: *How Much Bigger?*

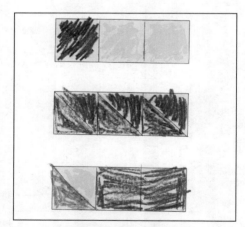

From: *Fraction Fill-Up*

With a roomful of children busily engaged in their investigations, it is not easy for a teacher to keep track of how individual children are working. Having tangible material to gather and examine when the time is right will help you to keep in close touch with each child's learning.

Exploring Tangrams

The Tangram is a deceptively simple set of seven geometric shapes made up of five triangles (two small triangles, one medium triangle, and two large triangles), a square, and a parallelogram. When the pieces are arranged together they suggest an amazing variety of forms, embodying many numerical and geometric concepts. The Tangram pieces are widely used to solve puzzles which require the making of a specified shape using all seven pieces. Cuisenaire's seven-piece plastic Tangram set comes in in four colors—red, green, blue, and yellow.

The three different-sized Tangram triangles are all similar, right isosceles triangles. Thus, the triangles all have angles of 45°, 45°, and 90°, and the corresponding sides of these triangles are in proportion.

Another interesting aspect of the Tangram set is that all of the Tangram pieces can be completely covered with small Tangram triangles.

small triangle	medium triangle	square	parallelogram	large triangle

Hence, it is easy to see that all the angles of the Tangram pieces are multiples of 45—that is, 45°, 90°, or 135°, and that the small Tangram triangle is the unit of measure that can be used to compare the areas of the Tangram pieces. Since the medium triangle, the square, and the parallelogram are each made up of two small Tangram triangles, they each have an area twice that of the small triangle. The large triangle is made up of four small Tangram triangles and thus has an area four times that of the small triangle and twice that of the other Tangram pieces.

Another special aspect of the pieces is that all seven fit together to form a square.

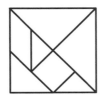

Some children can find the making of Tangram shapes to be very frustrating, especially if they are used to being able to "do" math by following rules and algorithms. For such children, you can reduce the level of frustration by providing some hints. For example, you can put down a first piece, or draw lines on an outline to show how pieces can be placed. However, it is important to find just the right level of challenge so that children can experience the pleasure of each Tangram investigation. Sometimes, placing some Tangram pieces incorrectly and then modeling an exploratory approach like the following may make children feel more comfortable: "I wonder if I could put this Tangram piece this way. I guess not, because then nothing else can fit here. So I'd better try another way...."

WORKING WITH TANGRAMS

Tangrams are a good tool for developing spatial reasoning and for exploring fractions and a variety of geometric concepts, including size, shape, congruence, similarity, area, perimeter, and the properties of polygons. Tangrams are especially suitable for children's independent work, since each child can be given a set for which he or she is responsible. However, since children vary greatly in their spatial abilities and language, some time should also be allowed for group work, and most children need ample time to experiment freely with Tangrams before they begin more serious investigations.

Young children will at first think of their Tangram shapes literally. With experience, they will see commonalities and begin to develop abstract language for aspects of patterns within their shapes. For example, children may at first make a square simply from two small triangles. Yet eventually they may develop an abstract mental image of a square divided by a diagonal into two triangles, which will enable them to build squares of other sizes from two triangles.

Tangrams can also provide a visual image essential for developing an understanding of fraction algorithms. Many children learn to do examples such as 1/2 = ?/8 or 1/4 + 1/8 + 1/16 = ? at a purely symbolic level so that if they forget the procedure, they are at a total loss. Children who have had many presymbolic experiences solving problems such as "Find how many small triangles fill the large triangles," or "How much of the full square is covered by a small, a medium, and a large triangle?" will have a solid intuitive foundation on which to build these basic skills and to fall back on if memory fails them.

Young children have an initial tendency to work with others, and to copy one another's work. Yet, even duplicating someone else's Tangram shape can expand a child's experience, develop the ability to recognize similarities and differences, and provide a context for developing language related to geometric ideas. Throughout their investigations, children should be encouraged to talk about their constructions in order to clarify and extend their thinking. For example, children will develop an intuitive feel for angles as they fit corners of Tangram pieces together, and they can be encouraged to think about why some will fit in a given space and others won't. Children can begin to develop a perception of symmetry as they take turns "mirroring" Tangram pieces across a line placed between them on a mat and can also begin to experience pride in their joint production.

Children of any age who haven't seen Tangrams before are likely to first explore shapes by building objects that look like objects—perhaps a butterfly, a rocket, a face, or a letter of the alphabet. Children with a richer geometric background are likely to impose interesting restrictions on their constructions, choosing to make, for example, a filled-in polygon, such as a square or hexagon, or a symmetric pattern.

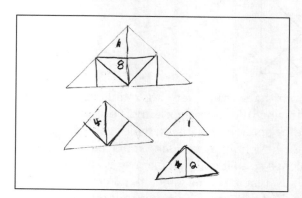

From: *Triangle Mania*

If you dubbled the size of the game and used more piees it would take longer to play but the same stratigy would still work. It is try and get rid of my big piees first because little ones can fit into more places.

From: *Shape Shut-Out*

ASSESSING CHILDREN'S UNDERSTANDING

The use of Tangrams provides a perfect opportunity for authentic assessment. Watching children work with the Tangram pieces gives you a visual sense of how they approach a mathematical problem. Their thinking can be "seen," in so far as that thinking is expressed through their positioning of the Tangram pieces, and when a class breaks up into small working groups, you are able to circulate, listen, and raise questions, all the while focusing on how individuals are thinking.

To ensure that children know not only how to do a certain operation but also how it relates to a model, assessment should include not only symbolic pencil-and-paper tasks such as "Find 1/2 + 1/8," but also performance tasks such as "Show why your answer is correct using Tangram pieces."

Having children describe their creations and share their strategies and thinking with the whole class gives you another opportunity for observational assessment. Furthermore, since spatial thinking plays an important role in children's intellectual development, include in your overall assessment some attention to spatial tasks.

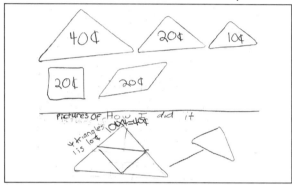

From: *Shopping for Shapes*

From: *Shopping for Shapes*

Models of teachers assessing children's understanding can be found in Cuisenaire's series of videotapes listed below.

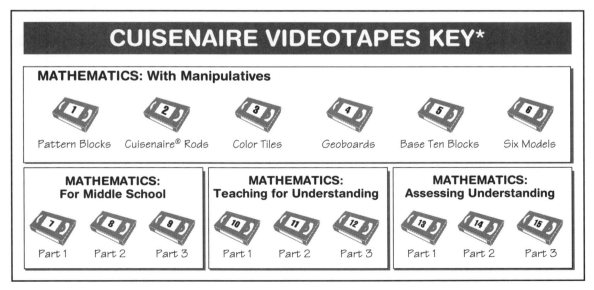

*See *Overview of the Lessons*, pages 16–17, for specific lesson/video correlation.

Connect the Super Source™ to NCTM Standards.

	PROBLEM SOLVING	COMMUNICATION	REASONING	CONNECTIONS	Geometry	Logic	Measurement	Number	Patterns/Functions	Probability/Statistics
CHANGING AREA UNITS	◆	◆	◆	◆	◆		◆		◆	
DESIGN IT WITH SYMMETRY	◆	◆	◆	◆	◆	◆				
FIELDS AND FENCES	◆	◆	◆	◆			◆			◆
FLIP-FLOP AROUND	◆	◆	◆	◆					◆	
FRACTION FILL-UP	◆	◆	◆	◆				◆		
FRACTION SPIN	◆	◆	◆	◆				◆		
HOW MUCH BIGGER?	◆	◆	◆	◆			◆		◆	
IT CAN BE ARRANGED	◆	◆	◆	◆					◆	
MAKE YOUR OWN TANGRAMS	◆	◆	◆	◆		◆	◆			
ONE CHANGE AT A TIME	◆	◆	◆	◆						
POLYGON PARADE	◆	◆	◆	◆						
SHAPE SHUT-OUT	◆	◆	◆	◆		◆				
SHOPPING FOR SHAPES	◆	◆	◆	◆	◆		◆	◆		
THE LONG AND SHORT OF IT	◆	◆	◆	◆			◆			
THE TAN-ANGLES	◆	◆	◆				◆			
THE TILE MAKER COMPANY	◆	◆	◆	◆			◆	◆	◆	
TRIANGLE MANIA	◆	◆	◆	◆	◆		◆	◆		
TWENTY QUESTIONS	◆	◆	◆	◆		◆	◆			

TOPICS

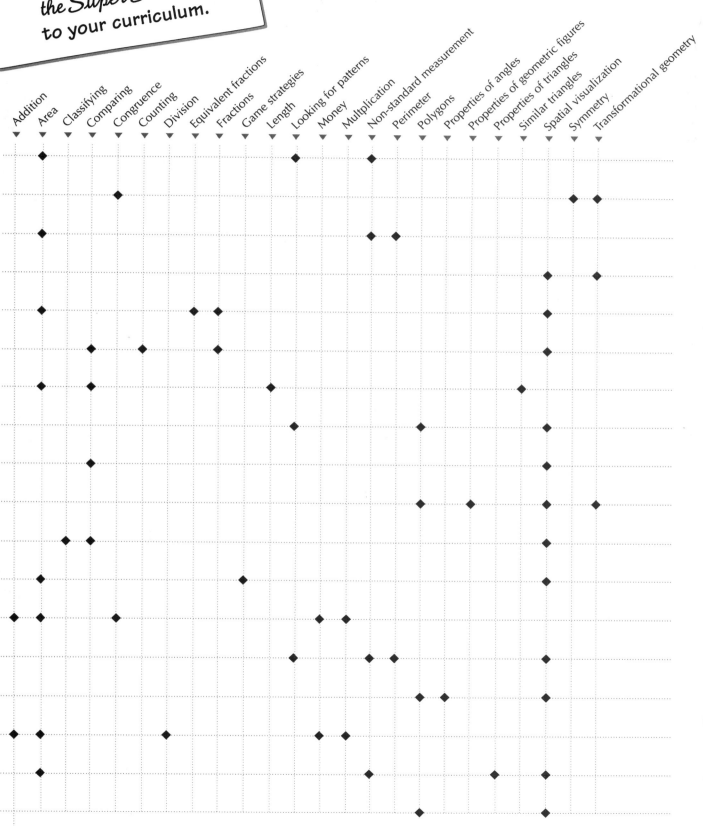

Addition
Area
Classifying
Comparing
Congruence
Counting
Division
Equivalent fractions
Fractions
Game strategies
Length
Looking for patterns
Money
Multiplication
Non-standard measurement
Perimeter
Polygons
Properties of angles
Properties of geometric figures
Properties of triangles
Similar triangles
Spatial visualization
Symmetry
Transformational geometry

More SUPER SOURCE™ at a glance:
TANGRAMS for Grades K-2 and Grades 5-6

Classroom-tested activities contained in these *Super Source*™ Tangrams books focus on the math strands in the charts below.

...the Super Source™ Tangrams, Grades K-2

Geometry	Logic	Measurement
Number	Patterns/Functions	Probability/Statistics

...the Super Source™ Tangrams, Grades 5-6

Geometry	Logic	Measurement
Number	Patterns/Functions	Probability/Statistics

Classroom-tested activities contained in these *Super Source*™ books focus on the math strands as indicated in these charts.

...the Super Source™ Snap™ Cubes, Grades 3-4

Geometry	Logic	Measurement
Number	Patterns/Functions	Probability/Statistics

...the Super Source™ Cuisenaire® Rods, Grades 3-4

Geometry	Logic	Measurement
Number	Patterns/Functions	Probability/Statistics

...the Super Source™ Geoboards, Grades 3-4

Geometry	Logic	Measurement
Number	Patterns/Functions	Probability/Statistics

...the Super Source™ Color Tiles, Grades 3-4

Geometry	Logic	Measurement
Number	Patterns/Functions	Probability/Statistics

...the Super Source™ Pattern Blocks, Grades 3-4

Geometry	Logic	Measurement
Number	Patterns/Functions	Probability/Statistics

Overview of the Lessons

See video key, page 11.

Tangrams, Grades 3-4

See video key, page 11.

CHANGING AREA UNITS

- Area
- Non-standard measurement
- Looking for patterns

Getting Ready

What You'll Need

Tangrams, up to 8 sets per group

Area Units worksheet, 1 per child, page 90

More Area Units worksheet, 1 per child, page 91

Overhead Tangram pieces, and/or *Area Units* and *More Area Units* worksheet transparencies (optional)

Overview

Children fill polygon outlines with Tangram triangles of each of three different sizes. In this activity, children have the opportunity to:

- ◆ use spatial visualization
- ◆ discover patterns that occur in collected data
- ◆ develop an understanding of equivalence

The Activity

Introducing

- ◆ Have children remove the different-sized triangles from a Tangram set and identify the three sizes: small, medium, and large.

- ◆ Ask children to make a square using the two large triangles. Display an outline of this square. Add a diagonal line to show a possible placement of the triangles.

- ◆ Now ask children to use their Tangram pieces to figure out how one could make two more squares of the same size, first from all medium triangles, and then from all small triangles.

- ◆ Have volunteers come up to the board to draw squares and add lines to them to show the placement of the medium and small triangles. Each time, have children count off the number of triangles that they would use.

- ◆ Elicit that two large, four medium, and eight small triangles can be used to build the squares of the same size.

On Their Own

How can you find the area of polygons using Tangram triangles?

- Work in a group of 3. Remove all the triangles from your Tangram sets. Make piles of small, medium, and large triangles. Each person in your group should take 1 pile.

- As a group, choose one of these polygons from your worksheets:

A   B   C   D   E   F   G

  Each of you should measure the area of that polygon by filling it with your triangles—the small ones, the medium ones, or the large ones.

- Decide on a way to record your findings.

- Trade piles of triangles and measure the area of another of the polygons. Try to measure it with all three sizes of triangles. Record your findings.

- Keep on trading, measuring, and recording until you have found the areas of all the polygons on your worksheets using triangles of all three sizes.

The Bigger Picture

Thinking and Sharing

Have volunteers discuss the various recording methods that they used. Prepare a class chart on the board. Then ask a volunteer to begin filling in the chart for recording polygon areas on the board. In the first column, *Polygon*, he or she should draw and label the first polygon, *A*, and then label three columns as *Small Triangles*, *Medium Triangles*, and *Large Triangles*.

If you do not wish to discuss fractional pieces of triangles at this time, use only the Area Units *worksheet with polygons A–C.*

Polygon	Small Triangles	Medium Triangles	Large Triangles
A			

Call on members of various groups to complete the chart by repeating this process for each remaining polygon. Then call on groups to contribute their data to fill in the chart.

Use prompts like these to promote class discussion:

- What patterns do you see in the chart?

- Did you ever think you knew the area of a polygon without measuring it? How did you know?

- Which size triangle was the easiest to use? the hardest?

- Could each polygon be filled with every size of triangle? Why or why not?

- Do you think you could use the Tangram square to measure the area of these polygons? Could you use the Tangram parallelogram? Why or why not?

Extending the Activity

Suggest that children use Tangrams to create their own polygons, then use the triangles of three sizes to measure the area of each. Have them add this data to their charts.

Teacher Talk

Where's the Mathematics?

In this activity, children investigate the area of polygons using non-standard units. As children explore the relationships among the sizes of Tangram triangles, they gain an informal understanding of equivalent fractions.

Even if children are working with the *Area Units* worksheet alone, recording data only for polygons A, B, and C, they will have enough information to see an emerging pattern of the triangle areas.

If children work with polygons A-G, they may observe that only Polygons A, B, and C can be covered with a whole number of large triangles. They will also find that only Polygons A, B, C, D, and E can be covered with a whole number of medium triangles, but that any one of the polygons can be covered with a whole number of small triangles.

The complete data chart shows the following:

Polygon	Small Triangles	Medium Triangles	Large Triangles
A	8	4	2
B	16	8	4
C	12	6	3
D	14	7	3½
E	10	5	2½
F	5	2½	1¼
G	11	5½	2¾

As children fill the outlines with Tangram pieces, some may have an intuitive spatial sense of the area of the pieces. They may visualize that the medium triangle covers the same area as do two small triangles and that the large triangle has an area equivalent to four small triangles.

Small triangle

Medium triangle

Large triangle

Other children use this relationship between the small triangle and each of the other triangles to find numbers to use as divisors when finding equivalent numbers of triangles for some of the polygons. For example, polygon G can be covered by 11 small triangles; 11 ÷ 2, or 5½ medium triangles; and 11 ÷ 4, or 2¾ large triangles.

Children who see the relationships among the three triangle sizes may be able to mentally find the area once an outline has been filled with one size of triangle. These children may be ready to work with more challenging polygons.

Some children may rely heavily on a substitution strategy to measure area. For example, once an outline has been filled with large Tangram triangles, these children may substitute two medium triangles for each large triangle, and then two small triangles for each medium triangle. Using these relationships, some children may use addition or multiplication to calculate the number of small, medium, or large triangles needed.

Polygon A filled
with 2 large triangles.

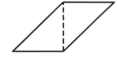

Thus, 2 x 2, or 4 medium triangles and 2 x 4, or 8, small triangles will fill Polygon A.

Sometimes, when children come upon a polygon that cannot be filled with a whole number of large or medium triangles, they may use a small triangle to fill in the extra space.

Polygon F   large triangle

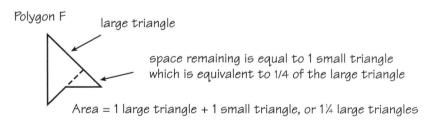

space remaining is equal to 1 small triangle which is equivalent to 1/4 of the large triangle

Area = 1 large triangle + 1 small triangle, or 1¼ large triangles

As they study the chart, the numerical relationships that children may notice will strengthen their understanding of fractions and the meanings of doubling and halving.

DESIGN IT WITH SYMMETRY

• Symmetry
• Congruence
• Transformational geometry

Getting Ready

What You'll Need

Tangrams, 2 sets in 2 different colors per pair

Symmetry Squares outline, several per pair, page 92

Crayons or markers (red, yellow, blue, green)

Mirrors

Overhead Tangram pieces and/or *Symmetry Squares* outline, transparency (optional)

Overview

Children make designs that have line symmetry by positioning two colors of Tangram pieces on a 10-cm square outline. In this activity, children have the opportunity to:

◆ understand the meanings of *horizontal*, *vertical*, and *diagonal*

◆ discover characteristics of symmetrical designs

◆ explore ways to create designs that have line symmetry

The Activity

Be sure children understand that the reflection they see in the mirror shows the matching part of the triangle, the part on the other side of the mirror, or line of symmetry.

Introducing

◆ Hold a large Tangram triangle against the chalkboard as shown and trace it.

◆ Now draw a vertical dotted line through the right angle vertex and say that the line is called a line of symmetry. Ask volunteers to tell how the line changes the triangle.

◆ Elicit that the line of symmetry separates the triangle into two matching parts.

◆ Have children put large Tangram triangles on their desks, orienting them the way you did. Demonstrate how to hold up a mirror on the triangle along the line of symmetry. Ask one or two children to peek into the mirror and to describe what they see.

◆ Challenge children to find four different lines of symmetry for the Tangram square. Help them position their mirrors on the square to find their solutions.

◆ Trace a Tangram square four times across the chalkboard. Call on volunteers to draw different lines of symmetry on the squares.

◆ Identify the lines as *vertical*, *horizontal*, and *diagonal*.

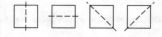

On Their Own

How can you create designs that have line symmetry?

- You and a partner need 2 different-colored Tangram sets and a square outline that looks like this one:

- Decide how you can make a Tangram design that fits within the square outline and has line symmetry. Here's how to check to be sure your design has line symmetry: Use a mirror. Hold it up along what you think is a line of symmetry. If you see the matching half of the design reflected in the mirror, your design has line symmetry.

Horizontal
line symmetry

Vertical
line symmetry

Diagonal
line symmetry

No line
symmetry

- Record your design, then cut out the square. Fold it along the line of symmetry. When you unfold it, check again that the two parts match exactly.

- On the back of your design, describe its kind of line symmetry. Write H (Horizontal), V (Vertical), D (Diagonal). If it doesn't have symmetry after all, write N (for no line symmetry).

- Make more symmetrical Tangram designs. Try to make at least one with each kind of symmetry. Record each design and cut it out.

The Bigger Picture

Thinking and Sharing

Write the column headings *Horizontal, Vertical, Diagonal,* and *No Line Symmetry* across the chalkboard. Call on pairs to post one of their designs in each of the four columns.

Use prompts like these to promote class discussion:

- What does the chart show?

- How can you tell if a design has symmetry?

- Did you use some Tangram pieces more often than others in your designs? Why?

- How did you tell if the line symmetry in a design was vertical, horizontal, or diagonal?

- Which kind of symmetry is easiest to see? Why?

Writing

Ask children to list three questions about line symmetry that could be answered by looking at the postings.

Extending the Activity

1. Have children repeat the activity, this time using more than two colors in their designs.

2. Challenge children to make designs that have turn symmetry. Use two paper squares of the same size to model quarter-turn symmetry and two paper parallelograms of the same size to model half-turn symmetry.

Teacher Talk

Children may use informal language or drawings to explain directionality.

horizontal

side-to-side
back and forth
going across

vertical

up and down
from top to
bottom
standing up

diagonal

corner-to-corner
kitty-corner
slantwise

Where's the Mathematics?

Exploring symmetry through this activity gives children the opportunity to visualize and identify geometric changes. Children may recognize types and directions of symmetry as classification attributes. They may also add to their geometry vocabulary as they talk about *horizontal*, *vertical*, and *diagonal symmetry*.

In the Introducing activity, some children may look for additional help with symmetry. Identifying designs that are not symmetrical may be as valuable as studying designs that are. Some children may view a vertical line as the only orientation for a line of symmetry. Other children may turn a design with vertical symmetry to prove that horizontal and diagonal symmetry exist. Some children may notice that a design can have more than one line of symmetry. You might want to model the following designs:

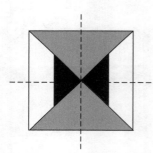

Two lines of symmetry
(horizontal and vertical)

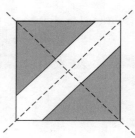

Two lines of symmetry
(on the diagonals)

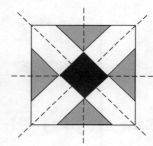

Four lines of symmetry

Children can check for symmetry in various ways. Some may eyeball the design, and some may fold the paper along the imaginary line. Others may use the side of their hand to divide the design.

Place one square over the other and push an opened paper clip through their centers. Hold the bottom square still as you turn the top one slowly, noting that the top square covers the bottom square four times, or makes four quarter-turns, in order to make a complete turn. Repeat the demonstration using the parallelograms, noting that the top one covers the bottom only after making a half-turn.

Some children may want to explore using the mirror to find the symmetry in other designs and objects in the classroom. They may observe that reflection causes a symmetrical image to appear.

Some children may observe that their designs actually consist of three colors: the two Tangram colors and the white background. Through experimenting, children may discover that the same design can have a different look when the three colors are interchanged as shown below.

  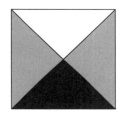

The designs shown here are typical of those that children may post on the class chart.

Vertical symmetry	Horizontal symmetry	Diagonal symmetry	No symmetry
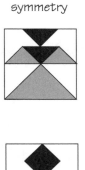	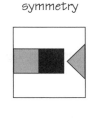		

FIELDS AND FENCES

- Area
- Perimeter
- Non-standard measurement

Getting Ready

What You'll Need

Tangrams, 2 sets per child

Number cube (marked 1-6) or die, 2 per pair

Small Tangram Triangles, 12 per group, page 93

Tangram Ruler, page 94, or centimeter ruler, 1 per group

Overview

Children build Tangram shapes to match an area designated by the roll of a pair of number cubes. Then they find the perimeter of the shape. In this activity, children have the opportunity to:

- ◆ express area as a number of small Tangram triangles
- ◆ express perimeter in centimeters
- ◆ explore the relationship between area and perimeter

The Activity

If children have had prior experience finding area, they may suggest multiplying to find the area. If you choose to discuss area more formally, be sure to have children suggest which standard unit of measure they would use to express it.

Introducing

- ◆ Display a recording of this shape made from the large Tangram triangle and the square.

- ◆ Demonstrate how to use a small Tangram triangle to measure the area of the shape, recording each small triangle as you position it.

- ◆ Elicit that, since it takes six small triangles to completely cover the shape, the *area* of the shape can be expressed as "six small triangles."

- ◆ Demonstrate how to measure each side of the shape in centimeters using a centimeter ruler. Record each measurement in centimeters.

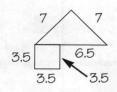

- ◆ Call on a volunteer to trace a path around the shape with a finger. Say that this distance is the perimeter of the shape.

- ◆ Elicit that the sum of the measures of the sides is 31 cm, so the *perimeter* of the shape can be expressed as "31 cm."

On Their Own

How much fencing would you need to go all the way around a "field" made from Tangram pieces?

- Have someone in your group roll 2 number cubes.

- Think of the sum of the numbers rolled as the number of small triangles that will exactly cover a Tangram shape.

- Choose Tangram pieces that together can be exactly covered by your number of small triangles.

- Each person in the group should use these same pieces to make a different shape, or "field."

- Compare your field with those made by others.

  - If they are different, record them.
  - If they are not different, agree on changes that will make them different. Then record your work.

- To know how much fencing you would need to enclose your field, find the perimeter of your field, or the distance around it. Write it on the field.

- Make a chart showing your group's fields. Write the perimeter of each field below it. Then write this sentence on your chart, filling in the sum you rolled:

  The area of our fields is _____ small triangles.

The Bigger Picture

Thinking and Sharing

Ask the groups to announce the sums they rolled for the areas of their fields. Write the numbers across the top of the chalkboard. Then have the groups post their charts below the corresponding numbers.

Use prompts like these to promote class discussion:

- How did you decide which Tangram pieces to use to make your fields?

- Why do you think more fields can be made for some areas than for others?

- How many different sums could you have rolled using the two number cubes? How do you know?

- What do you notice about the perimeters of different fields made with the same Tangram pieces?

Extending the Activity

1. Assign groups the perimeter of a field, such as 19 cm, 24 cm, or 28 cm. Direct them to use small triangles to build a field with that perimeter. Then have them express the area of their field as a number of small triangles.

Teacher Talk

Where's the Mathematics?

The concepts of area and perimeter are usually presented separately to children. By investigating both area and perimeter together as done in *Fields and Fences,* children make comparisons and discover relationships between these concepts while developing spatial and reasoning skills.

Using the small triangle to find area gives children experience using non-standard units of measure. As an alternative to using the Tangram ruler or centimeter ruler to find perimeter, children may be allowed to use a small Tangram triangle. (The short side of the small triangle is 3.5 cm long. The long side measures 5 cm.)

Children can roll sums of 2 to 12. Some may notice that it is more likely to roll certain sums than others. From prior experience rolling a pair of dice, children may observe that 7 comes up the most frequently, followed by 6 and 8, 5 and 9, 4 and 10, 3 and 11, then 2 and 12.

You may want to engage children in creating a chart like this one to display the 21 possible number combinations (or areas of fields) that can be rolled on a pair of number cubes, or dice, and the sums of these combinations:

NUMBERS ROLLED	1-1	1-2	1-3	1-4	1-5	1-6	2-2	2-3	2-4	2-5	2-6
SUM	2	3	4	5	6	7	4	5	6	7	8

NUMBERS ROLLED	3-3	3-4	3-5	3-6	4-4	4-5	4-6	5-5	5-6	6-6
SUM	6	7	8	9	8	9	10	10	11	12

If a group rolls a low number, the variety of Tangram pieces and the shapes they can make will be limited. Children may discover that using as many small Tangram triangles as possible gives them the most flexibility in making different shapes.

Children with little or no experience in measuring area with small triangles may have to measure the pieces individually before deciding which to use. Children who have worked with these non-standard measurements before may recall that each piece has an area equal to the following numbers of small triangles:

Square, parallelogram, or medium triangle = 2 small triangles
Large triangle = 4 small triangles

2. Have children repeat the activity using manipulatives such as Color Tiles or one kind of Pattern Block. Be sure they understand that the area of their fields should now be expressed in terms of this new unit of measure.

Group's charts may look like the one shown here:

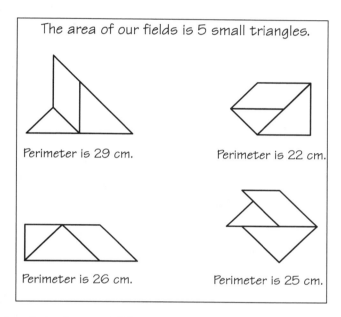

The area of our fields is 5 small triangles.

Perimeter is 29 cm.

Perimeter is 22 cm.

Perimeter is 26 cm.

Perimeter is 25 cm.

In comparing their charts, children may notice that the variety of shapes increases as the area number increases.

Children will discover that shapes with the same area do not necessarily have the same perimeter. They may also see that the more compact a shape is the shorter the perimeter. Some children may extend this abstract observation further, finding that the closer a shape approximates a square, the smaller its perimeter. These children are beginning to understand that, for a given area, the polygon with the least perimeter is always a square. For example, a group might roll an area of eight, and choose to represent it with a large triangle and two medium triangles. If the following fields are built, children should note that the square field has the least perimeter.

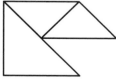

A = 8 small triangles
P = 38 cm

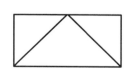

A = 8 small triangles
P = 30 cm

A = 8 small triangles
P = 28 cm

FLIP-FLOP AROUND

- Spatial visualization
- Transformational geometry

Getting Ready

What You'll Need

Tangrams, 1 set per child

Flip-Flop cards, 1 set per group, page 95

Flip-Flop game board, 1 per child per game, page 96

Crayons or markers (red, yellow, blue, green)

Overhead Tangrams and/or *Flip-Flop* game board transparency (optional)

Overview

Children use Tangrams to play a game in which pieces undergo transformations. In this activity, children have the opportunity to:

- explore slides, flips, and turns
- use the language of transformational geometry
- investigate combinations of transformations

The Activity

Although mathematically a shape can be slid in any direction, for the purpose of preparing children for the Flip-Flop game, we are suggesting that they get used to sliding their Tangram pieces only horizontally and vertically.

You may want to have children practice making turns, slides, and flips with other Tangram pieces until they understand and can demonstrate the meaning of each word.

Introducing

- Mark an arrow on a piece of unlined paper, hold it in this position against the chalkboard, and say that the arrow is pointing upward:

- Slide the paper across the board and say that this shows a *slide*. Rotate the paper so that the arrow is pointing to the right and say that this shows a *turn*. Flip the paper so that the arrow cannot be seen and say that this shows a *flip*.

- Challenge children to use a large Tangram triangle to model a slide, a flip, and a turn.

- Have a volunteer model the slide and point out that a slide moves the triangle from side to side or up and down.

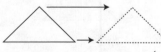

- As another child models the flip, explain that the triangle can be flipped along any one of its sides.

- As a third child models the turn, elicit that the triangle should be held in place, then carefully turned around one of its corner points or vertices.

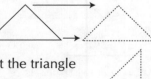

On Their Own

Play Flip-Flop!

Here are the rules:

1. This is a game for 2 to 4 players. The object is to be the first to get all the way across the game board.

2. Players each place a square Tangram piece on their own Flip-Flop game board so it fits in one corner like this:

3. Players trace their Tangram pieces in their starting positions. They color the tracings to match the pieces.

4. Players mix up a set of *Flip-Flop* cards and place them face down. Then players decide who will go first.

5. The first player picks a card and moves his or her Tangram square according to these rules:

   • SLIDE: slide the square 1, 2, or 3 spaces in any one direction.

   • FLIP: flip the square on one of its sides in any direction.

   • TURN: turn the square in any direction using a corner of the square as the turning point.

6. The player records the move by tracing and coloring the Tangram square in its new position.

7. Players take turns picking cards, moving their squares, and recording the moves. The player who gets to the opposite side of his or her game board first wins.

• Play *Flip-Flop* again. This time, use a different Tangram piece!

• Be ready to talk about good moves and bad moves.

The Bigger Picture

Thinking and Sharing

As children declare "a win", suggest that the members of each group compare their game boards to see how they all moved their squares. Then post one group's game boards.

Use prompts like these to promote class discussion:

◆ Can you tell by looking at a game board which cards the player picked? How do you know?

◆ Was it easier to slide, flip, or turn your square? Why do you think this was so?

◆ Which kind of move was most helpful in winning the game?

◆ How did you decide how far to turn a piece?

◆ How did you decide in which direction to flip a piece?

◆ Which Tangram pieces were the easiest to move? Which were the hardest to move?

Drawing

Have children create a design using one Tangram piece. Allow them to choose the piece, then slide, flip, or turn it, tracing the piece in each new position. Most children will want to color their designs.

Where's the Mathematics?

This activity uses Tangram pieces to give children a concrete experience in transformational geometry. The use of the *Flip-Flop* game board, actually 0.5-cm graph paper, prepares them for later activities involving coordinate geometry.

As children place their Tangrams on the grid and perform the transformations, they may notice that the square was the easiest piece to move on the game board and often looked the same no matter how it was moved. Some children may realize this is because the square is symmetrical and so its appearance does not change when it is slid, flipped, or rotated at 90°, or one-quarter intervals.

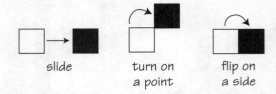

slide   turn on a point   flip on a side

The most difficult piece for most children to move across the game board is the parallelogram because it does not have reflective (line) symmetry and has rotational symmetry only when it undergoes a 180° turn or half turn.

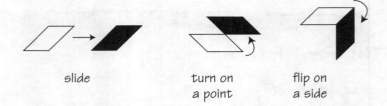

slide   turn on a point   flip on a side

Depending on the starting position of a piece, many children can turn and slide the triangles with little difficulty. Only when they flip the piece do children have to take notice of the long and short sides of the triangle or the right angle and the 45° angles.

slide   turn on a point   flip on a side

Extending the Activity

1. In this version of the game, the winner is the player who can keep playing the longest. No play can overlap a previous play. Players must try to strategize to keep from blocking their next moves.

2. Have children play the game again, but this time on each turn, a player draws two cards and chooses which one to play. After the piece is moved, both cards are put in a discard pile. When there are no more cards, the discard pile is shuffled and play continues until one player's Tangram piece reaches the other side.

To describe a *slide*, children may use the words *up, down, left, right, above,* and *below*. To describe a *flip*, children may talk about the *side* or *point* on which they flipped the piece. If children think about flipping a pancake or piece of paper, they may choose to flip so that the center of the piece remains in the same place on the game board. Some children may realize that this kind of flip does not help them achieve their objective of reaching the other side of the game board.

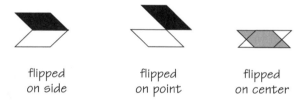

| flipped on side | flipped on point | flipped on center |

To describe a *turn*, children may refer to the direction of the turn as going *to the left* (counterclockwise) or *to the right* (clockwise). Other children may be more precise as they state the fractional amount of the turn (*quarter turn, half turn.*) Children are likely to find that the center point of a turn makes a difference. Here are some designs using quarter turns. The turn center (center of rotation) is different in each case.

| quarter turn to right | half turn on center | half turn to left |

During the activity, children will have some exposure to the concept of orientation. As they work, children may see that slides preserve the original orientation of any Tangram piece while flips and turns do not necessarily preserve a piece's orientation.

FRACTION FILL-UP

- • Spatial visualization
- • Meaning of fractions
- • Equivalent fractions
- • Area

Getting Ready

What You'll Need

Tangrams, 4 sets in 4 different colors per pair

Crayons or markers (red, yellow, blue, green)

Fraction Fill-Up Rectangles worksheet, page 97, 1 per pair

Overhead Tangram pieces and/or *Fraction Fill-Up Rectangles* transparency (optional)

Overview

Children use Tangram pieces of different colors to represent fractional parts of shapes. In this activity, children have the opportunity to:

- ◆ write a fraction to represent part of a whole
- ◆ explore fractional equivalence
- ◆ discover size relationships among Tangram pieces

The Activity

You may want to point out that the dotted line divides the large triangle into halves, or two equal parts.

Point out that these dotted lines divide the large triangle into quarters, or four equal parts.

Introducing

- ◆ Trace a large Tangram triangle on chart paper. Hold two medium triangles on the tracing to show how it can be filled exactly.
- ◆ Draw a dotted line on the tracing to show how the medium triangles covered the large triangle. Write ½ next to each part.
- ◆ Trace three large Tangram triangles across the chart. Ask a child to fill one of them exactly with small Tangram triangles. Draw dotted lines to show how the small triangles fit. Write ¼ next to each part.
- ◆ Draw the same dotted lines on the next two large triangles. Invite a child to color three quarters of one of them. Ask someone else to do this another way. Point out that the colored sections need not touch.

- ◆ Trace three more large triangles. Have children cover them exactly using small triangles and a square, a parallelogram, and a medium triangle. Have them draw lines and color three quarters of each triangle.

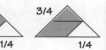

On Their Own

How can you use Tangrams to show fractional parts of a rectangle?

- You and your partner need 4 different Tangram sets and a worksheet that looks like this one:

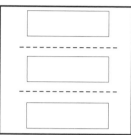

- Use Tangram pieces to fill up the first rectangle outline. Make it ½ red and ½ blue. Trace the pieces in place on the outline. Then color to record your work.

- Fill up the second rectangle with Tangram pieces. Make this rectangle ⅓ blue and ⅔ yellow. Trace the pieces and color the outline.

- Fill up the third rectangle so that it is ⅙ yellow, ⅙ green, and ⅔ red. Trace the pieces and color the outline.

- Cut along the dotted lines on your worksheet to separate your rectangles. Be ready to tell how you figured out how to fill each one.

The Bigger Picture

Thinking and Sharing

Write these three column headings on the chalkboard: ½ red and ½ blue, ⅓ blue and ⅔ yellow, and ⅙ yellow, ⅙ green, and ⅔ red. Have pairs post their rectangles in the corresponding columns.

Use prompts like these to promote class discussion:

- What do you notice about all the rectangles?

- How did you go about "filling up" the outlines with Tangram pieces?

- How are some of the combinations of Tangram pieces the same? How do some of them differ from the others?

- Which fractional part of a shape covers more space, one half or one quarter? How do you know?

- What fractional part of this rectangle does each color represent? How do you know?

- Suppose you made a rectangle in which the small Tangram triangle represented *one eighth* of a whole. Would the rectangle be smaller, larger, or the same size as the rectangles used in this activity?

Extending the Activity

Prepare a worksheet with triangle and trapezoid outlines having the dimensions shown. Distribute three copies of the worksheet to each pair.

10 cm   10 cm   14 cm   7 cm   7 cm   10 cm   14 cm

Where's the Mathematics?

As children search for fractional and geometrical combinations to fill rectangular outlines, they gain a concrete understanding of the meaning of fractions, fractional equivalence, and how parts relate to the whole. They may also draw conclusions about area. Children have the opportunity to become more familiar with geometric properties of shapes, which may increase their knowledge of relationships among Tangrams. In order to find workable solutions, they practice spatial visualization and logic skills.

In the Introducing activity, in order to show three quarters of the large triangle, some children may suggest changing the positions for the Tangram pieces, realizing that the solution still works.

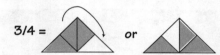

Some children may insist that a color does not represent a fraction unless the pieces are touching. Some children may need to substitute other Tangram pieces or rearrange the pieces to see the relationship between the pieces and the fractions they represent.

Children should notice that a small triangle covers half of the medium triangle, half of the square, and half of the parallelogram. In their search for solutions, children may choose to use the small triangle as a basis for measurement of area.

As they plan strategies, children may note that Tangram pieces do not have to be the same shape to represent the same fractional part. Although the fractional parts are the same size, they may be made from different numbers and kinds of Tangram pieces. For example, in the figure below, children may recognize that one third can be represented by two small triangles, one parallelogram, or one square.

R G R B

1/3 =   1/3 =   1/3 =

Challenge children to fill up the outlines, recording their work, to show these fractional parts of the two figures:

Triangle:
¾ yellow and ¼ red
½ yellow and ⅜ green
½ blue, ¼ yellow, and ¼ red

Trapezoid:
⅔ green and ⅓ yellow
½ red and ½ green
¾ blue and ¼ red

Children may use many different approaches as they begin to fill up their rectangle outlines. Some may begin with the largest Tangram pieces, then try to make the smaller pieces fit. Others may try pieces randomly. Still others may make combinations that are equivalent to certain fractions and then try to fit them within the outline. A child may even fill in the rectangle with Tangram pieces and then color the rectangle in order to represent a Tangram piece. For example, the figure below shows how a child used the four small triangles from two Tangram sets, then drew another small triangle to represent five sixths.

Some possible ways to fill the *Fraction Fill-Up Rectangles* are:

½ red, ½ blue

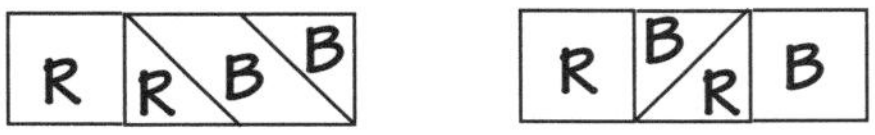

⅓ blue, ⅔ yellow

⅙ yellow, ⅙ blue, ⅔ red

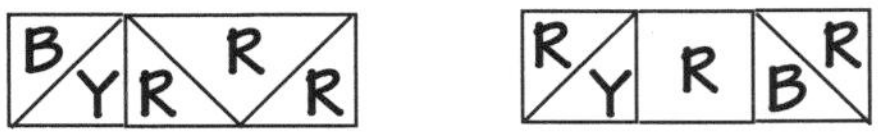

FRACTION SPIN

- Spatial visualization
- Fractions
- Counting
- Comparing

Getting Ready

What You'll Need

Tangrams, 1 set per group

Fraction Spinner, 1 per group, page 98

Small paper clip, 1 per group

Overhead Tangram pieces (optional)

Overview

Children identify a Tangram piece as a fractional part of a whole shape. Then they construct the whole. In this activity, children have the opportunity to:

- ◆ count fractional parts to make a whole
- ◆ compare fractional parts according to area
- ◆ learn that the denominator of a fraction is the number of parts that make up a whole
- ◆ understand the relationship between the numerator and the denominator of a fraction

The Activity

Introducing

- ◆ Make the shape shown with three large triangles, but keep it hidden.

- ◆ Tell children you are hiding a shape that was made from only large Tangram triangles and that the shape is smaller than a sheet of notebook paper. Ask children to guess how many large triangles you used.

- ◆ Write down all the guesses.

- ◆ Now, give the class the following clue: The large triangle is one third of the whole shape.

- ◆ Ask children to guess again, this time giving a reason for their guesses. Then, reveal the shape.

Tell children that the number below the bar, or denominator, in any fraction always tells how many parts of the same size are in the whole.

- ◆ Fill the shape with large triangles. Establish that "three" is the only possible solution because one third or ⅓ means "one out of three equal parts."

On Their Own

> **What can you find out about a whole shape if a Tangram piece stands for a fraction of that shape?**
>
> - Work with a group. Each of you should choose one Tangram piece.
>
> - Take turns spinning the Fraction Spinner.
>
> - What fraction did you spin? Use that fraction as the value of your Tangram piece.
>
> - Figure out how many of your pieces you would need to make a whole shape. Arrange, or trace, that many pieces so they form a shape you like.
>
> - Record your shape. Label each piece with its fractional value.
>
> Here is an example.
>
>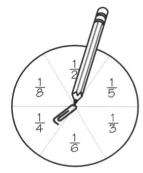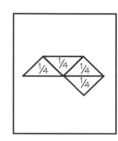
>
> - Compare the shape you made with those of your group.
>
> - Repeat the process for other spins of the spinner.
>
> - Be ready to explain what you noticed.

The Bigger Picture

Thinking and Sharing

Begin a class chart by posting the fractions ½, ⅓, ¼, ⅕, ⅙, and ⅛ across the chalkboard. Invite volunteers, one at a time, to post their shapes under the proper heading. Ask them to name the piece they used to build their whole shape and tell how many of them make up the whole.

Use prompts like these to promote class discussion:

- What do you notice about the postings?

- How did you know how many pieces to use?

- Look at all the shapes in the column labeled ———. How are they the same? How are they different? How do they compare to the shapes in the other columns?

- Are shapes with the same number of pieces always the same size? Explain.

Where's the Mathematics?

A big idea in fractional work is that the whole, or 1, is not always the same size or made up of the same number of pieces. Comparing and contrasting shapes where the same unit fraction has been assigned to different Tangram pieces helps children to develop this understanding.

As they first look at the class postings, children usually make two observations. One is that the number of pieces in a shape matches the denominator of the assigned fraction. The other is that shapes made with the same number of equal-sized pieces do not have to look alike. For example, here are some possible solutions children may find for the fraction ⅕.

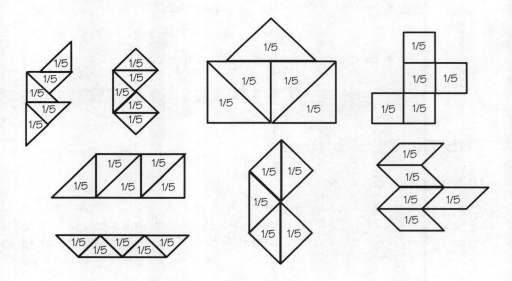

Writing and Drawing

Ask children to explain, with words and pictures, why each of the fractions ²⁄₂, ³⁄₃, and ⁴⁄₄ is equal to 1.

Extending the Activity

1. Create a set of task cards. Ask children to repeat the activity, but this time have them draw only the outline of their shape. Then ask them to write the following directions above their shapes: If my shape is equal to 1 write a fraction for each Tangram piece. Have them put the answers on the other side of the paper.

By counting or adding the pieces in every whole shape children discover that each is equal to ⁸⁄₈. Most of the shapes do not look alike. However, it is, possible to have similar shapes, that is, shapes that look exactly alike but are of different sizes. The seven-sided figures above are identical in shape but one is made with small triangles and the other with medium triangles.

When comparing the postings in different columns, children may notice that it is possible to have congruent shapes that are made from different pieces, as are the three squares shown below. One square is made up of Tangram squares and shows ¼. Another square, also showing ¼, is made with medium triangles. Still another square is made with small triangles and shows ⁸⁄₈.

Physically arranging multiples of the same piece into a whole helps children understand the meaning of a fraction; that is, for example, that ⅛ means "one out of eight equal parts" or that ³⁄₃ means "three out of three equal parts."

HOW MUCH BIGGER?

• Comparing
• Length
• Area
• Similar polygons

Getting Ready

What You'll Need

Tangrams, 2 sets per pair

Small Tangram Triangles, 16 per pair, page 93

Big and Bigger worksheet, 1 per child, page 99

How Much Bigger? worksheet, 1 per pair, page 100

Tangram ruler, page 94, or centimeter ruler

Overhead Tangram pieces and/or *Big and Bigger* and *How Much Bigger?* worksheet transparencies (optional)

Overview

Children use small triangles to measure and compare Tangram pieces to similar polygons. In this activity, children have the opportunity to:

◆ explore the relationship between the lengths of the sides of similar polygons

◆ compare areas of similar polygons

◆ discover patterns and use them to make predictions

The Activity

You may want to use overhead Tangrams or paper Tangrams to display the shapes shown on the worksheets.

You may want to point out that any two polygons that have the same shape, but not necessarily the same size, are similar to each other. Some children may also realize that corresponding angles of similar polygons are equal.

Introducing

◆ Distribute copies of the *Big and Bigger* worksheet.

◆ Cover the triangle outline at the top of the page with a large Tangram triangle and tell children to do the same.

◆ Lead a discussion about how this triangle outline is like the one below it and how it is different.

◆ Elicit that the two triangles are alike in that they both have two sides of equal length and one longer side and that they each have one square corner.

◆ Establish that the only difference between the triangles is size.

◆ Then point out that the two triangles are *similar* because they are exactly alike, except for size.

◆ Ask children how they might find out how much bigger one triangle is than another. Discuss children's responses and record their suggestions.

On Their Own

How can you use Tangram pieces to find out how much bigger one polygon is than another?

- Work with a partner. Share a *How Much Bigger* worksheet that looks like this:

- Put these Tangram pieces on the outlines of your worksheet where they fit exactly.

Square   Medium Triangle   Parallelogram

- Measure the area of the Tangram square with small Tangram triangles. Write the area on the Tangram square outline.

- Decide how you can measure the area of the similar, larger square. Measure it and write the area on the larger square outline.

- Do the same for the medium Tangram triangle and the larger triangle, and again for the Tangram parallelogram and the larger parallelogram.

- Be ready to tell how much bigger each larger shape is than the similar, smaller one.

The Bigger Picture

Thinking and Sharing

Ask pairs if any of them marked the larger outlines showing how they found the area of these shapes. Have any pairs who did post their work.

Use prompts like these to promote class discussion:

- ◆ How does the length of a side of a small shape compare to the length of the corresponding side of the similar, large shape?

- ◆ How did you measure the area of each large shape?

- ◆ How does the area of each large shape compare with the area of the similar, small shape?

- ◆ What patterns do you see between the similar shapes? between each of the pairs of shapes?

Extending the Activity

1. Have children make a shape from any two Tangram pieces. Then have them double the sides of that shape to make a larger shape. Have them predict the area of their new shape, measure the area with small triangles, and record it.

Where's the Mathematics?

As children compare the lengths of two shapes of different sizes, they begin to understand the concept of similarity. As they measure area informally using small triangles, they may draw conclusions about the relationship between perimeter and area.

In order to compare lengths of the sides of each pair of similar shapes, most children will move each small shape around the larger, similar shape, marking off the number of repetitions of the shorter side along each corresponding longer side.

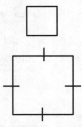

Alternately, children may use the sides of a small Tangram triangle to measure the lengths of the sides of each pair of similar shapes.

In order to compare areas of each pair of similar shapes, most children will position the smaller shape within a corner of the larger, similar one, flipping it across and up or down as many times as necessary to cover the entire region. Some children who have done this may trace the small piece as they move it into each new position. You may want to suggest that children who have done this demonstrate this method for any pairs who seem unable to discover their own way of finding area.

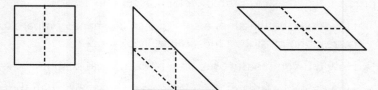

Other children will cover each pair of shapes exactly with small triangles, then count and record the number needed to cover each.

Children may believe that when the lengths of the sides of a shape are doubled, the area will also double. These children may be surprised to find the area of the larger shape is four times the area of the smaller shape. As children discover this, they may begin calculating the area by multiplying instead of measuring with small triangles.

2. Ask children to choose a Tangram piece and use it to draw a similar shape with sides that are three or four times longer. Have them predict the area of the new shape and then measure and express the area as a number of small triangles.

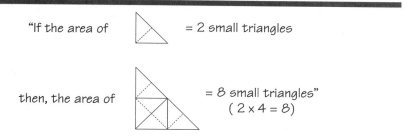

"If the area of ◺ = 2 small triangles

then, the area of ◺ = 8 small triangles"
(2 x 4 = 8)

Below are the solutions for creating similar polygons with double the side lengths for each of the Tangram pieces. The area of each piece, expressed as a number of small triangles, is shown in parentheses.

	Actual size	With Sides Doubled
Small Triangle	(1)	(4)
Medium Triangle	(2)	(8)
Large Triangle	(4)	(16)
Square	(2)	(8)
Parallelogram	(2)	(8)

IT CAN BE ARRANGED

- Spatial visualization
- Properties of polygons
- Looking for patterns

Getting Ready

What You'll Need

Tangrams, 4 triangles of the same size per pair

Tangram Tracing Paper, several sheets per pair, page 101

Small Tangram Triangles, page 93 (optional)

Medium and Large Tangram Triangles, page 102 (optional)

Overhead Tangram pieces and/or Tangram paper transparency (optional)

Overview

Children make as many different polygons as they can using four Tangram triangles of the same size. In this activity, children have the opportunity to:

- classify polygons according to their number of sides
- recognize differences in polygons

The Activity

This might be the time to discuss how to tell whether two polygons are the same or different. Point out that generally, polygons are considered to be the same if, through a combination of slides, flips, or turns, they can be made to look the same.

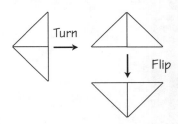

Introducing

- Display the following shapes made from two of the same-sized Tangram triangles.

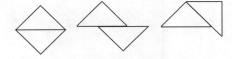

- Ask children which of the shapes is made up of triangles whose edges match completely.

- Invite a volunteer to use the same two triangles to make a different shape with sides that match completely. Then ask another volunteer to do the same.

- Ask children how they know the three shapes differ.

- Explain that closed shapes like these whose sides are made up of line segments that meet to form angles are called *polygons*.

On Their Own

How many different shapes can you make from the same Tangram triangles?

- With a partner, predict how many different polygons can be made using 4 Tangram triangles of the same size.

- Make a polygon using the 4 triangles. Make sure that the edges that touch match exactly.

- Put your polygon on Tangram tracing paper. Trace it and cut it out.

- Take turns making, tracing, and cutting out different polygons.

- Compare your polygons. If any two are congruent, or match exactly when flipped or turned, keep only one of them.

- Be ready to discuss how you figured out how to make a new polygon.

The Bigger Picture

Thinking and Sharing

Ask children to suggest ways of grouping the shapes they have made. They may suggest: according to the number of sides, types of angles, and number of lines of symmetry. Allow children to decide on a preferred way. Then write column headings on the chalkboard to reflect their decision. Invite each pair to post one of their shapes in the appropriate column. Have them continue posting shapes until several of each kind of shape has been posted.

Use prompts such as these to promote class discussion:

- What kinds of polygons did you make?

- Which polygons have square corners, or right angles? How can you describe some of the other angles of your polygons?

- What special names do some of the angles and polygons have?

- How did you check a new polygon to see if it was different from one you already made?

- How else could you have sorted the polygons? What chart-headings would you then need?

- Do you think all the shapes that can be made with four triangles have been posted? Explain.

Extending the Activity

1. Have children predict and then show the shapes that can be made from three Tangram parallelograms.

2. Have children predict and then show the shapes that can be made from four Tangram squares.

Where's the Mathematics?

As children work through this activity, they explore polygons with different numbers of sides and different kinds of angles.

Children may notice that by lining up the edges of two or more triangles it is possible to create a single side of a shape. For example, the bottom edge of the trapezoid below is made by lining up the edges of three Tangram triangles. When counting the number of sides of the polygon, children may need to be reminded that the sides of Tangrams forming straight lines are counted as one side. Thus, in the case of the trapezoid below, the shape has four sides.

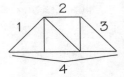

During the process of making the shapes, children may search for words to talk about new geometric concepts. Model the correct use of these vocabulary words: congruence, parallelogram, quadrilateral, and trapezoid.

After making each shape, children may use different strategies to check to see that the shape is a new solution. Some children may place the tracings of previous solutions onto the new shape and then slide, flip, or turn it to see if they match. Other children may trace and cut out the new shape before comparing with previously obtained solutions. Still other pairs may turn, slide, or flip the new shape before tracing to see if it matches any previous solution. Children are likely to encounter some matches as they work. For example, the sixteen figures below are all flips or turns of a single polygon.

Children may suggest a variety of ways to group their shapes. Some of the possibilities are:

◆ according to number of sides – 3, 4, 5, or 6

◆ according to number of lines of symmetry – 0, 1, 2, 3, or 4

◆ according to kinds of angles (right angles or no right angles, and so on)

Children may have difficulty finding all the four-triangle shapes. They may be surprised at how many different possible solutions there are:

MAKE YOUR OWN TANGRAMS

- Spatial visualization
- Comparing
- Following directions

Getting Ready

What You'll Need

Tangrams, 1 set per child

Tangrams in a Square worksheet, 1 per group, page 103

Construction paper (8-in. square), 1 piece per group

Overhead Tangram pieces and/or *Tangrams in a Square* transparency (optional)

Overview

Children make their own Tangram set by folding and cutting a square piece of paper. In this activity, children have the opportunity to:

- ◆ look for relationships between geometric figures
- ◆ develop an understanding of fractional equivalence
- ◆ write and follow directions

The Activity

In the On Their Own *activity, some children may want to use plastic Tangram pieces to cover the* Tangrams in a Square *diagram before they begin to fold or cut.*

Introducing

- ◆ Ask children to put the medium Tangram triangle and the two small Tangram triangles together to form a square.
- ◆ Have them put their square on a piece of paper, trace around the edge of it, then cut it out.
- ◆ Tell children that you want to cut the same three Tangram pieces from this square without tracing them.
- ◆ Model one possible strategy, by first folding the square in half along one diagonal and then along the other. Then show children how you can trace over some fold lines so that you have the outline of the medium Tangram triangle and the two small Tangram triangles.

Fold   Trace

- ◆ Position plastic Tangram pieces over your paper square to show children how to check your work.

On Their Own

How can you make your own set of paper Tangrams?

- Work in a group using the *Tangrams in a Square* outline sheet. Talk about how you might divide this square to get the 7 Tangram pieces without tracing the pieces on the square.

- Make a plan. Talk about ways you could fold your square to mark the places to cut. Decide what to do first, second, and so on.

- Now follow the group's plan to fold and cut your paper square. If the plan is not working, talk to your group about ways to change it.

- When you have cut out the Tangram pieces, make sure that they can be fit together again to form a square.

- With your group, write a list of directions for cutting a set of Tangram pieces from a square. Be sure to label your directions Step 1, Step 2, and so on.

- Be ready to talk about how you decided on your plan for making your Tangram set.

The Bigger Picture

Thinking and Sharing

Ask one child from each group to read his or her group's directions to the class.

Use prompts like these to promote class discussion:

- How were the lists of directions the same? How were they different?

- How did you use the *Tangrams in a Square* outline to help you make your Tangram set?

- How did you choose which line to fold or cut first?

- Which pieces were the easiest to fold? Which were the most difficult?

- Did you try a step that did not work? If so, what did you do?

- Would following your group's directions using a much larger square also get you the seven Tangram pieces? Explain.

Writing and Drawing

Have the same groups rewrite their directions using drawings and numbers only. Suggest that children develop and use symbols that would tell the reader when to fold and/or cut.

Where's the Mathematics?

In this activity, as children explore geometric properties they begin to develop an understanding of the relationship among Tangram pieces. This lays a foundation for higher level experiences with fractional equivalence and measurement.

Children may use different methods of making a set of Tangram pieces. Some may fold and cut each piece individually. Some may try to cut out shapes without folding, approximating the size and shape of pieces. Some may fold the entire square to make a grid of triangles and then cut out the pieces.

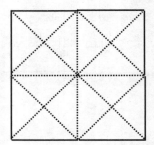

Children who begin by folding and cutting the square into two triangular halves may then fold one in half again to make the two largest Tangram triangles. Children will then be challenged to make the other five pieces from the remaining half.

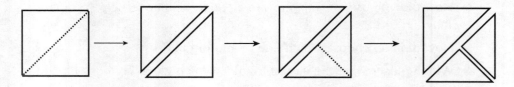

The five pieces can be made by folding down the right-angle vertex of the triangular half so that it touches the center of the hypotenuse. Cutting along the fold line produces the medium Tangram triangle and a large trapezoidal piece.

Extending the Activity

Have groups exchange lists and follow each other's directions to cut out Tangram sets from 8-inch-square pieces of construction paper. Have children talk about whether or not the directions worked and if necessary how any directions should be changed.

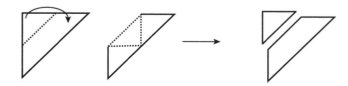

Folding the trapezoid in half, then making two more folds, produces the square, parallelogram, and two small triangles.

Some children may check their work by comparing their cut-out pieces with the plastic Tangrams. Other children may compare the relationship between pieces. For example, they may check the size of the parallelogram by covering it with two small triangles. Children may also talk about the fractional representations of the whole shape, noting, for example, that a large Tangram triangle equals one quarter of the completed *Tangrams in a Square* outline. Some may note the area relationships within the shape. For instance, they may say that the small triangle is half the size of the small square or half the size of the parallelogram.

Groups may record their directions in a variety of ways. Some may choose to write their directions on a square piece of paper or on the *Tangrams in a Square* outline, numbering the order in which to fold along the lines. Others may make a list of numbered steps, recording them in great detail in short phrases or with drawings only. Encourage groups to talk about their strategies. By sharing directions, children build their mathematical vocabulary and learn to better understand the relationships among the Tangram pieces.

ONE CHANGE AT A TIME

- **Spatial visualization**
- **Polygons**
- **Transformational geometry**
- **Properties of geometric figures**

Getting Ready

What You'll Need

Tangrams, 1 set per child

Overhead Tangrams (optional)

One Change at a Time Cards, pages 104-105 1set per group

Overview

Starting with a Tangram square, children try to move only one piece to make polygons that fit a particular description. In this activity, children have the opportunity to:

- ◆ expand their mathematical vocabulary
- ◆ make and identify a variety of polygons
- ◆ compare and contrast polygons
- ◆ use slides, flips, and rotations to transform shapes
- ◆ improve spatial reasoning

The Activity

Introducing

- ◆ Ask children to make a triangle with the two small Tangram pieces and the square. Then display yours.

- ◆ Now tell children to change the triangle to a rectangle by moving only one piece. Confirm there is only one way to do this.

- ◆ Have children make the triangle again. Then, moving only one piece, ask children to make a pentagon or 5-sided shape.

- ◆ Invite volunteers to describe or draw their pentagons.

- ◆ Establish that there is more than one way to do this.

On Their Own

> ## What shapes can you make with the 3 smallest Tangram triangles?
>
> - Work with a group. Each of you should take 2 small triangles and 1 medium triangle.
>
> - Place the stack of *One Change at a Time* cards face down. One of you picks a card and reads it aloud.
>
> - Follow these steps to decide if it is possible or impossible to make the shape.
>
>   - Start with a Tangram square that looks like this:
>   - Move only one piece so that all or part of a side of each piece touches the side of another piece.
>
>   Okay   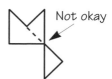 Not okay
>
>   - Compare your shapes.
>
>   If they are different, record them.
>
>   If they are the same, record only one.
> - Repeat the process for each of the cards.
> - Be ready to discuss your observations and discoveries.

The Bigger Picture

Thinking and Sharing

Have groups take turns sharing their solutions and posting them until there are samples of each of the shapes that are possible to make.

Use prompts like these to promote class discussion:

- What did you notice while trying to make each shape?
- Which shapes were the easiest to make? the hardest? Why?
- What do you notice when you look at the posted shapes?
- Which shapes were impossible to make? Why?
- Which shapes fit into more than one category?
- Which shapes can be made in only one way? In just two ways? In more than two ways?

Extending the Activity

1. Have children repeat the activity, this time starting with a rectangle or a parallelogram.

2. Have children repeat the activity but use 5 pieces or 7 pieces to make the starting shape.

3. Have children create new cards to add to the set of *One Change at a Time Cards*.

Where's the Mathematics?

This activity helps children build their mathematical vocabulary and gives them an opportunity to bring meaning to the words. Children sharpen their visualization skills as they search for each shape. Comparing the shapes allows children to internalize definitions and create mental images. It is often surprising to children to learn that octagons do not have to look like "stop signs" or that not all quadrilaterals have symmetry.

Ten of the shapes can be made in at least one way. The remaining six are impossible. These include the rectangle, the square, the quadrilateral with no parallel sides, the convex pentagon, and the decagon. Although the three pieces in the starting square can make a rectangle, it requires moving more than one piece. The square is often debated. Some may argue that by flipping one of small triangles and replacing it, they have formed a "new" square. The only other quadrilateral that can be made is the parallelogram; though many pentagons can be made, none can be made without indents. And the most sides that any polygon can have is eight, making the decagon impossible.

Here are some examples of the shapes that are possible to make following the rules of the activity. The shaded piece was the one that was moved.

Starting
Square

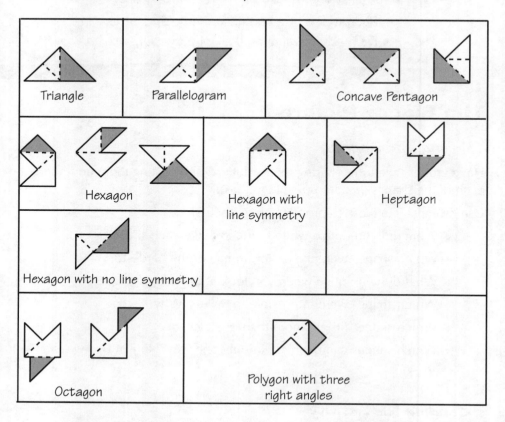

Triangle   Parallelogram   Concave Pentagon

Hexagon   Hexagon with line symmetry   Heptagon

Hexagon with no line symmetry

Octagon   Polygon with three right angles

Most children begin making shapes using trial and error, sliding, rotating, or flipping a piece. As they experiment, discuss what they've made, and refer to their recordings, children can become better at visualizing and often move a piece to verify their mental image. Some begin to see patterns. For example, to make an octagon, either the two small triangles must be separated or one of the triangles must be placed so that its vertices do not touch those of the piece it is aligned with.

In discussing the activity, even if children ignore the rules they often come up with ideas that help sharpen their visual acuity. One such example is sequentially transforming the figures from a square to a parallelogram then to a rectangle and finally to a triangle.

Another discovery is noticing that extending a side, completely covering a side, or leaving part of a side exposed affects the total number of sides.

6 sides   7 sides   8 sides

POLYGON PARADE

- Spatial visualization
- Comparing
- Classifying

Getting Ready

What You'll Need

Tangrams, 1 set per child

Newsprint or construction paper,1
11 x 17-in. piece per group

Crayons or markers, red, yellow, blue,
and green

Overhead Tangram pieces (optional)

Overview

Children build polygon shapes using different numbers of Tangram pieces.
They record their results on a shape chart. In this activity, children have the
opportunity to:

◆ explore the characteristics of polygons

◆ apply spatial visualization

◆ develop an understanding of relationships among polygons

The Activity

*Some children may say that they
made the square another way. If they
do, draw another square on the board.
Ask a volunteer to draw a dotted line
on it to show the other way—a
diagonal line connecting the other two
corners.*

Introducing

◆ Have children remove the two small triangles from their Tangram
sets. Tell them to use the two pieces to make a square. Record a
square on the chalkboard.

◆ Invite a volunteer to model how to form the square from the two
small triangles. Be sure all children understand how to do this.

◆ Draw a dotted line diagonally on the square to show how
the two small triangles can make up the square.

◆ Now challenge children to use the two small triangles to
make two other shapes—a triangle and a parallelogram. Draw the
outlines of these polygons on the chalkboard as you name them.

◆ Call on volunteers to come to the board to draw dotted lines on
these shapes to show how they formed each of them from the two
small triangles.

On Their Own

How can you use Tangram pieces to make different polygon shapes?

- Working in a group, make a chart like this one on a large sheet of paper.

- Take the 3 smallest triangles from a Tangram set. Use them all to make a square.

	square	triangle	rectangle	parallelogram
3 smallest triangles				
5 small pieces				
all 7 pieces				

- Draw a square on your chart in the space where the first row and the first column meet. Then draw dotted lines on your square to show how you placed the 3 triangles.

- Use the same triangles to make 3 more shapes—a triangle, a rectangle, and a parallelogram. Draw each shape, then draw dotted lines on each to record.

- Now, make each of the 4 shapes again, using the 5 smaller pieces from your Tangram set (all but the 2 large triangles). Record your work on the chart.

- Keep going. This time, use all 7 Tangram pieces to make each shape! Record your work on the chart.

- Be ready to talk about how you decided to make the polygon shapes from different numbers of Tangram pieces.

The Bigger Picture

Thinking and Sharing

Have children post their charts on the board.

Use prompts like these to promote class discussion:

- What did you discover about the way the Tangram pieces fit together?

- Which polygons were the easiest to make? Which were the hardest? Why?

- Why is it sometimes possible to find more than one way to make a polygon?

- How did knowing how to make one polygon help you make another?

Extending the Activity

1. Explain that a trapezoid is a four-sided polygon with two parallel sides. Challenge children to build trapezoids using three small pieces, the five small pieces, then all 7 Tangram pieces. You may want to have children start by adding this column head to their charts:

trapezoid

2. Have children explore building six-sided shapes (hexagons) using three small pieces, the five small pieces, and all seven pieces in their Tangram sets.

Where's the Mathematics?

To make this an on-going learning activity, you may want to provide a classroom polygon chart. Children may add new solutions to the chart as they discover them.

While building polygons using three, five, and seven Tangram pieces, children use problem-solving skills to demonstrate their understanding of the characteristics of polygons. As children work, some may notice that the lengths of the sides of all polygons are multiples of the short and long sides of the small triangle. They may use this fact to match similar edges.

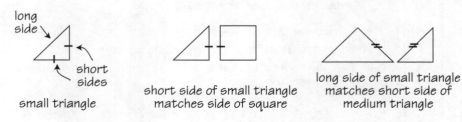

Children may discover that there is more than one way to make each of the polygons. This becomes clear as they flip and rotate pieces and when they substitute some pieces for others having the same area. A few samples are shown here.

	square ▢	triangle ◺	rectangle ▭	parallelogram ▱
3 smallest triangles				
5 small pieces				
all 7 pieces				

While manipulating Tangram pieces, some children may transform one solution into another by moving a piece or two. For example, here a child has changed the square made from the 3 smallest triangles into a parallelogram, a rectangle, and a triangle by moving only one piece at a time.

Here are some of the possible ways to build trapezoids and hexagons from various numbers of Tangram pieces.

	trapezoids
3 small pieces	
5 small pieces	
all 7 pieces	

	hexagons
3 small pieces	
5 small pieces	
all 7 pieces	

SHAPE SHUT-OUT

- Spatial visualization
- Area
- Game strategies

Getting Ready

What You'll Need

Tangrams, 2-4 sets in different colors per group

Shape Shut-Out game board, 1 per group, page 106

Overhead Tangram pieces and/or *Shape Shut-Out* game board transparency (optional)

Overview

In this game for two to four players, children take turns placing Tangram pieces on a game board in an effort to put down the last piece. In this activity, children have the opportunity to:

- manipulate Tangram pieces to fit them on a grid
- observe the way Tangram pieces can be combined into a rectangular configuration
- develop strategic thinking skills

The Activity

For a piece to fit on the game board, every side of the Tangram piece must align with a grid line. You may want to use overhead Tangrams to demonstrate how to place pieces correctly.

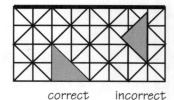

correct   incorrect

Introducing

- Display and distribute a *Shape Shut-Out* game board to each group. Tell children that they will be taking turns placing Tangram pieces on the board so that the pieces fit exactly within the grid lines.
- Ask volunteers to place one of each kind of Tangram piece on the board to show how each fits exactly.
- Challenge children to work together to fit two sets of Tangram pieces of different colors on the top half of the game board.
- Some children may suggest that each set can be put together to complete the large Tangram square puzzle on each half of the top of the board.

On Their Own

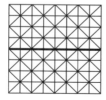

Play Shape Shut Out!

Here are the rules:

1. This is a game for 2 to 4 players. The object is to place the last Tangram piece on a game board that looks like this one. With only 2 players, only the top half of the game board is used. With 3 or 4 players, the whole game board is used.

2. Each player chooses 1 color of Tangram pieces. Players decide who will go first.

3. Players take turns placing a piece wherever it fits exactly on the game board.

4. The winner is the player who puts down the last piece.

• Play several games of Shape Shut-Out.

• Be ready to talk about good moves and bad moves.

The Bigger Picture

Thinking and Sharing

Invite children to talk about their games and describe some of the thinking they did.

Use prompts such as these to promote class discussion.

◆ Which Tangram pieces were the most difficult to play? Why?

◆ For each round, was it best to be the first to play? the last? somewhere in the middle?

◆ What moves changed the course of the game?

◆ What are some strategies for winning this game?

◆ Do you think all the players could use the same strategy in one game? Why or why not?

Writing

Ask children to respond to this question: "If you could double the size of the *Shape Shut-Out* game board and use twice as many pieces to play, do you think your strategy would still work or not?"

Extending the Activity

1. Have children use a five-sectioned spinner on which the five different Tangram pieces are pictured. On a turn, children should spin in order to determine which piece to put down on the grid.

Teacher Talk

You may want to point out that the large Tangram piece is positioned correctly on the grid when its longer side is either horizontal or vertical (and not diagonal) and when it covers eight (and not nine) of the small triangle grid sections.

Where's the Mathematics?

As children take turns placing their Tangram pieces on the *Shape Shut-Out* game board, they explore game strategies. Children use logic as they evaluate the space remaining on the game board and plan future moves.

As they play, children may observe that some Tangram pieces can only fit in certain ways on the grid. For example, the square must be turned with the vertex pointing upwards, and the longer side of the medium triangle must be oriented diagonally. Here is an expanded game board showing how the Tangram pieces can be placed.

To do well at the game, children may realize that they must think not only about fitting a piece on the board but also how to use the remaining space. Children may notice that a space can appear to be the right size, yet the piece may not fit when placed within the grid lines.

Children may discover that the most versatile Tangram piece is the one with the smallest area—the small triangle. Children may develop strategies in which they play larger pieces first and save the small triangles to play late in the game.

Multiple pieces from several sets could serve a common "pot" from which all players remove pieces.

2. Ask children to design a different kind of game board on which to play *Shape Shut-Out*.

As children look for winning strategies, some may begin to notice which pieces other players have left to play. Children may realize that once a player has no small triangles remaining, that player can be eliminated from play by positioning pieces to break up open spaces so that only small spaces remain.

If children play in pairs, some may discover that the second player can always win if he or she copies the first player's moves, playing the identical Tangram piece in a position that is one half turn rotation of the first player's move, as shown below.

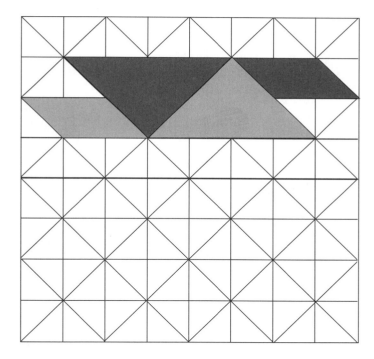

As children continue to explore game strategies, they may find that the same strategy will not help them win every time. As players pick up each other's strategies, they may find that the strategy that worked in the last game will no longer ensure a win. *Shape Shut-Out* encourages children to analyze each position anew and adapt strategies as they encounter new game situations.

SHOPPING FOR SHAPES

GEOMETRY • NUMBER • MEASUREMENT

- Addition
- Multiplication
- Money
- Congruence
- Area

Getting Ready

What You'll Need

Tangrams, 1 set per child

Small-Triangle Spinner page 107, 1 per group

Small paper clip, 1 per group

Overhead Tangram pieces (optional)

Overview

Children assign a monetary value to the small Tangram triangle. Based on this amount, they use Tangram pieces to make shapes equal in value to an amount spun on a spinner. In this activity, children have the opportunity to:

◆ apply strategies for adding and multiplying amounts of money

◆ develop the understanding that any shape made from Tangram pieces has an area equal to some number of small triangles

The Activity

In the On Their Own, *children may substitute 10 index cards for the spinner and write each multiple of the small triangle's price on a card. If children use the spinner, they may benefit from examining a filled-in spinner before they make their own.*

Demonstrate how to straighten one end of a paper clip, then how to use the point of the straightened end to pierce the center of the spinner. The part of the clip that lies flat on the spinner serves as the pointer.

Introducing

◆ Ask children to remove a small triangle and a medium triangle from a Tangram set. Have them compare the pieces and tell how they differ.

◆ Tell children to pretend that the small triangle costs 10¢. Based on this, ask them to give the cost of the medium triangle.

◆ Elicit that since the medium triangle is two times, or twice, the size of the small triangle, it costs twice as much as the small triangle, or 20¢.

◆ Now have children put a large Tangram triangle together with a small one to make this shape:

◆ Challenge children to give the cost of this shape based on the 10¢ cost of the small triangle. Have them explain their thinking.

On Their Own

How can you make a Tangram shape that costs a certain amount?

- With your group, decide on a cost for a small Tangram triangle. Choose any amount from 2¢ to 10¢.

- Make a spinner based on the cost you chose. Write your cost above the words "cost of 1" on a spinner that looks like this:

- What is the cost of 2 of your small triangles? the cost of 3? Write those amounts in the next sections on the spinner.

- Keep going around the spinner, writing the costs for up to 10 of your small triangles.

- Now spin! What amount did you spin? Use your Tangram pieces to make a shape that costs that amount.

- Record your shape. Write its cost on the recording.

- Repeat this process so that every one has a chance to spin.

- Be ready to explain how you made sure that your shape cost the amount you spun.

The Bigger Picture

Thinking and Sharing

Set up a chart by writing the possible costs for the small triangle, 2¢ to 10¢, across the top of the chalkboard. Then, call on groups to post their recordings in the column corresponding to the cost of their small triangle.

Children may want to arrange the shapes in each column by cost; for example, from least to greatest.

Use prompts such as these to promote class discussion:

- How are the shapes in a column alike? How are they different?

- Why do some shapes that cost the same look different?

- If you know the cost of the small Tangram triangle, how can you find the cost of the large Tangram triangle?

- If you were told the cost of the large triangle, how could you find the cost of the other pieces?

- Could the smaller of two shapes ever have the greater cost? Explain.

- How would you find the cost of each piece within a shape if you knew the cost of the whole shape?

Drawing

Point out that, each time children spin this spinner, they have an equally likely chance of spinning the costs of from 1 to 10 small triangles. Ask children to draw a spinner on which they would have equally likely chances of spinning the costs of only from 1 to 4 small triangles.

Where's the Mathematics?

In *Shopping for Shapes* children explore area relationships among Tangram pieces. While applying strategies of adding and multiplying prices based on the value of the small Tangram triangle, children may begin to understand the concept that shapes with the same area have the same cost.

As children fill in the sections on the spinner with multiples of the cost of the small Tangram triangle, they should make the connection that the shapes they make will also be related to the area of the small triangle. Children who know that it takes four small triangles to cover a large triangle may realize that they have only to multiply the cost of the small triangle by four to get the cost of the large one. For example, if the cost of the small triangle is 3¢, children may realize that a shape worth 24¢ costs eight times more and so must be eight times larger than one small triangle. In this situation, children might first make a shape with eight small triangles and then substitute larger pieces for some of the small triangles to create their final shape.

First shape   Final shape

Children may explore making a wide variety of shapes for some of the greater multiples they spin. For example, here are some solutions for making a shape that is priced at 24¢, when the cost of the small triangle is 3¢.

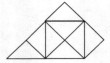
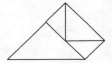
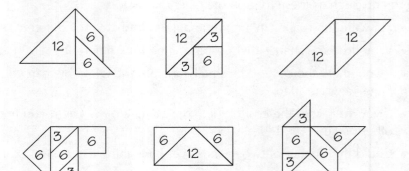

Extending the Activity

Have children make a shape using any four Tangram pieces. Then have them record the shape and write a total cost based on a chosen value for the small Tangram triangle.

Some children may use the strategy of writing an addition sentence for the amount they spin, then substituting pieces to match the sentence. In these examples, the cost for the small Tangram triangle is 5¢ and the value spun for the cost of eight small triangles is 40¢.

$$40¢ = 20¢ + 10¢ + 5¢ + 5¢ \qquad 40¢ = (3 \times 10¢) + (2 \times 5¢)$$

As children compare their shape outlines with those made by others, they may discover that shapes with the same area cost the same when the cost of the small triangle is the same. When the cost of the small triangle differs, however, the same shape is worth different amounts. In the following examples, the cost of the same shape is based on the small triangle values of 2¢, 3¢, 5¢, and 12¢ respectively.

Small triangle costs 2¢.

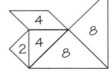

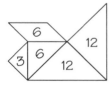

Small triangle costs 3¢.

Small triangle costs 5¢.

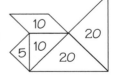

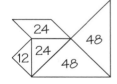

Small triangle costs 12¢.

Finding prices based on a unit rate (the price for the small Tangram triangle) helps children gain a better understanding of the relationship of a fractional part to the whole and prepares them to solve problems involving ratio and proportion.

THE LONG AND SHORT OF IT

- Perimeter
- Non-standard measurement
- Looking for patterns
- Spatial visualization

Getting Ready

What You'll Need

Tangrams, 1 set per child

Small Tangram Triangles, 10 per child, page 93

Overhead Tangram pieces (optional)

Overview

Children use the long and short sides of the small Tangram triangle as units of measure to find the perimeter of the Tangram pieces. In this activity, children have the opportunity to:

◆ discover relationships among the lengths of the sides of Tangram pieces

◆ measure length with non-standard units

◆ choose an appropriate non-standard unit of measure

The Activity

Introducing

◆ Display a drawing of a 15-cm (approximately 6-in.) line segment, but do not tell the class how long it is.

◆ Invite children to guess its length by estimating how many of the long sides of the small Tangram triangle fit along the line. Prove that three of the long sides fit by lining up small triangles as shown.

◆ Ask children if the length will be the same if one of the short sides of the small triangle is used to measure the line. Establish that a little more than four of one of the short sides fit.

◆ Show children that the line is also about as long as 3 short sides and one long side.

On Their Own

> ## What is the perimeter of each Tangram piece?
>
> - Pick a Tangram piece. The distance all the way around its edges is its *perimeter*. Trace the perimeter with your finger.
>
> - Now measure the perimeter of your piece with the sides of a small Tangram triangle. You can use the short side, the long side, or a combination of both. For example:
>
>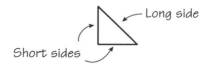
>
> Short sides
>
> Long side
>
> Small Tangram triangle perimeter =
> 1 long side and 2 short sides
>
> - Trace your Tangram piece and record its perimeter.
>
> - Repeat this process of finding and recording perimeter with each of the different Tangram pieces.
>
> - Arrange the pieces in order from the one with the least perimeter to the one with the greatest.
>
> - Be ready to report your findings and describe how you found the perimeter of each piece.

The Bigger Picture

Thinking and Sharing

Ask children which Tangram piece has the least perimeter and how they expressed it. Then invite volunteers to describe how they found the perimeter of that piece. Do the same for each of the remaining four pieces.

Use prompts like these to promote class discussion:

- What do you notice about the perimeters of the different Tangram pieces? Did anything about them surprise you?

- How did you decide when to measure in "longs" and when to measure in "shorts"? How did you decide when it was a good idea to use a combination of long and short sides?

- How do the side lengths of the small and large triangles compare? What did you notice about the lengths of the sides of these pieces?

Extending the Activity

1. Have children work in pairs to write length comparison questions such as, "Which is longer, three longs or four shorts?" Children can then trade questions with other pairs and use their Tangram pieces to find the answers.

Where's the Mathematics?

This activity provides children with concrete experience in using non-standard units of measure. As they make judgments about whether to use the long or short sides of Tangram pieces ("longs" or "shorts") to measure in each instance, they develop spatial visualization skills.

Below is a chart showing some of the solutions children might come up with. The perimeter, or distance around the Tangram pieces, was measured using short and long sides of the small Tangram triangle.

Tangram Piece	Longs	Shorts
small triangle	1	2
medium triangle	2	2
	3 ½	–
large triangle	2	4
	5	–
square	–	4
parallelogram	2	2

Deciding whether to measure with long or short sides is easiest when each side of the Tangram piece is equal to no more than one short or one long. Some children may use a trial-and-error approach, placing the short side first and choosing the long side if the short side does not work. Other children may be able to visualize a side as being equal to one long or one short. When a Tangram piece has two or more sides of equal length, some children may add or multiply to find the total distance around.

1 short x 4 = 4 shorts

There are only four different lengths for the sides of Tangram pieces. Every side is a long, a short, or double one of those. Children may invent the terms "double-long" and "double-short" for the two longest measurements.

Children may use different strategies to keep track of their work as they measure. Some children may leave the small triangles in place as they measure around the other Tangram piece. Once all of the sides are covered, these children count the number of long and short sides used.

2. Have children use Tangram rulers or centimeter rulers to measure the distance around each Tangram piece to the nearest half centimeter.

 2 shorts + 2 longs

Some children may trace the small triangle sides around the piece or ask to use paper Tangrams to measure. Others may make tick marks to show how the small triangle sides fit around the Tangram piece.

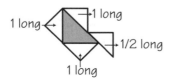 4 shorts + 2 longs

That none of the different pieces have the same perimeter may surprise the children who assumed that shapes with the same number of sides, like the square and the parallelogram, have the same perimeter. Others may even be surprised that the large triangle has a greater perimeter than the square since it has fewer sides than the square.

Children who prefer to use a single unit for each perimeter must do some mental estimation. For example, the two shorter sides of the medium triangle are equal to 1 long unit each. The third side is equal to 1 long and about ½ of another long, making the perimeter 3 ½ long units.

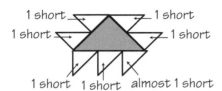

Measuring the large triangle in shorts means accepting that the longest side is just a bit shorter than three shorts.

Besides conceptualizing the meaning of perimeter through this activity, children also learn more about the Tangram pieces. For example, they may learn that every Tangram piece has at least two sides that are the same length and that each side of the large triangle is twice as long as the corresponding side of the small triangle.

THE TAN-ANGLES

- **Properties of angles**
- **Polygons**
- **Spatial visualization**

Getting Ready

What You'll Need

Tangrams, 1 set per child

Overhead Tangrams (optional)

Clock faces with movable hands (optional)

Overview

Children make a variety of Tangram shapes, then count and identify the angles, using a right angle as the benchmark. In this activity, children have the opportunity to:

- ◆ make and compare a variety of polygons
- ◆ notice how the sides and angles of a polygon are related
- ◆ determine if an angle is smaller, larger, or the same size as a right angle

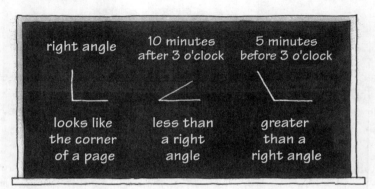

right angle	10 minutes after 3 o'clock	5 minutes before 3 o'clock
looks like the corner of a page	less than a right angle	greater than a right angle

The Activity

Some children may point out that the hands of the clock form two angles. If so, help them identify each one as smaller than, larger than, or the same size as a right angle.

This angle is smaller than a right angle.

This angle is larger than a right angle.

Introducing

- ◆ Ask children to draw four clock faces, showing 2 o'clock, 3 o'clock, 4 o'clock, and 7 o'clock respectively, while you do the same at the board.
- ◆ Explain that the figure formed by the two hands of the clock is called an *angle* and that angles come in many sizes. Draw an arrow on each clock face to show an angle (see below).
- ◆ Below the 3 o'clock drawing write "right angle." Point out the square corner. Illustrate by placing the Tangram square between the hands. Explain that all angles with square corners are called *right* angles.
- ◆ Ask children to decide which drawings show angles smaller than a right angle and which show angles larger than a right angle.
- ◆ Verify each identification by testing it with the Tangram square.
- ◆ Label each of the drawings as shown.

Smaller than a right angle.

Right angle

Larger than a right angle

Larger than a right angle

On Their Own

How big are the angles of a Tangram shape?

- Work with a partner. Pick a Tangram piece and count how many angles it has.

- Decide if each angle in the piece is smaller, larger, or the same size as a right angle. Record your findings.

- Do this for each of the other Tangram pieces.

- Now, you and your partner should each choose 2 or more Tangram pieces. Each of you use your pieces to make a shape you like. Be sure that a side of each piece is touching a side of another piece.

 Okay   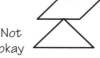 Not okay

- Record your shapes and the following information:
  - the number of sides in your shape
  - the number of angles in your shape
  - which angles are right angles
  - which angles are smaller than a right angle
  - which angles are larger than a right angle

- Compare your shapes and make a list of what you notice.

The Bigger Picture

Thinking and Sharing

Ask if anyone made a shape with fewer than three sides, then discuss why not. Ask if anyone made a shape with three sides. Have those children post their shapes. Next invite volunteers who made shapes with four sides to post their shapes. Continue with five sides, six sides, and so on until everyone has posted their shapes and all agree there are no duplicates.

Use prompts like these to promote class discussion:

- What kind of angles does the small Tangram triangle have? the square? the parallelogram? the medium triangle? the large triangle?

- How did your shape compare to your partner's?

- Which angles were the hardest to figure out? the easiest? Why?

- What do notice about the shapes that are posted?

- Is it possible to have shapes with no right angles? with one right angle? two? three? only right angles?

Extending the Activity

1. Have children sort their shapes in other ways, such as right angles/no right angles, symmetry/no symmetry, parallel sides/no parallel sides, perpendicular sides/no perpendicular sides.

Teacher Talk

Where's the Mathematics?

This activity gives children the opportunity to build mental images of different-size angles and establish the right angle as a benchmark for estimating the size of any angle. Children should develop visual images of angles before they are taught the mathematical names associated with angles to measure angles in degrees. This assures that learning that mathematicians call an angle less than 90° *acute,* an angle greater than 90° *obtuse,* an angle equal to two right angles *straight,* and an angle bigger than two right angles *reflex,* is simply attaching new names to a concept children are already familiar with. Having a mental image of a right angle makes it easier to understand how to use a protractor and to recognize that the end product when drawing a 150° angle cannot look like this:

There are only three different-sized angles in the Tangram set—a right angle, a smaller angle that is half the size of a right angle, and a larger angle that is one and a half times the size of a right angle.

The parallelogram has two of the smaller angles and two of the larger angles. The square has four right angles, and all of the triangles have one right angle and two smaller angles. Children are often surprised that the angles in the small Tangram triangle exactly match the angles in each of the other two triangles, even though the triangles themselves are not the same size.

From the posted shapes, children can conclude that the number of sides in a polygon is always the same as the number of angles. They should also conclude that it is possible for a shape to have no right angles. Some may notice that all the three-sided shapes are always triangles and that none have more than one right angle.

2. Explain that angles are measured in degrees and that a right angle has 90°. Then have children figure out the number of degrees in each angle of each of the Tangram pieces.

3. Have children find the total number of degrees in each Tangram piece and in the shapes they made.

It takes time for children to become skilled both at recognizing an angle in a shape and how it compares to a right angle. Often the orientation of an angle creates some difficulty. Have children who are having such difficulty, draw clock faces with times like these: 10 minutes after 9, 5 minutes before 9, and 30 minutes after 3. Then help them identify each one as less than, greater than, or equal to a right angle.

Children may describe *reflex* angles, angles greater than two right angles, as angles in corners (marked with arrows below) and may find them particularly hard to identify.

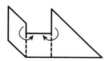

8 sides
8 angles
no right angles
3 smaller
5 larger

8 sides
8 angles
1 right angle
3 smaller
4 larger

9 sides
9 angles
2 right angles
2 smaller
5 larger

7 sides
7 angles
3 right angles
1 smaller
3 larger

8 sides
8 angles
5 right angles
none smaller
3 larger

6 sides
6 angles
1 right angle
2 smaller
3 larger

7 sides
7 angles
2 right angles
2 smaller
3 larger

THE TILE MAKER COMPANY

- Area
- Addition
- Multiplication
- Division
- Money

Getting Ready

What You'll Need

Tangrams, 3 sets (blue, red, green), per pair

Crayons or markers

Tile Maker Company Price Chart, 1 per pair, page 108

Calculators (optional)

Overview

Children design tile patterns and compute their cost based on the number, size, and color of Tangram pieces. In this activity, children have the opportunity to:

◆ explore area relationships among Tangram pieces

◆ look for numerical patterns

◆ develop strategies for figuring total cost

The Activity

Introducing

◆ Ask children where they have ever seen tiles used to decorate a home or a building. Talk about some places in which we use tiles: in the bathroom or kitchen, in a school or office building, on walls and/or on floors.

◆ Tell children to imagine that they are working for the Tile Maker Company. The company makes patterns of all shapes and sizes using tiles of three colors. The cost of a pattern depends upon the size, shape, and color of each tile piece.

◆ Give children a *Tile Maker Company Price Chart.* Ask them to read the chart to find the price of the small blue triangle, the medium red triangle, and the large green triangle. Make sure children understand that a tile that is twice as big as another costs twice as much.

◆ When you are sure everyone knows how to read the chart, ask children what they notice about the prices of the medium triangles compared to the prices of the small triangles. Ask why the medium triangles cost twice as much as the small ones. Ask children to suggest why one color tile might cost more than another.

Have children cover the medium triangle with two small triangles to verify that its area is twice as large.

On Their Own

How can you be a designer for the Tile Maker Company?

- With a partner, choose any 12 pieces from your three Tangram sets.

- Put the 12 pieces on a sheet of paper. Move them around to make a tile pattern. At least one complete side of each piece must touch a complete side of another piece.

- One of you should hold the pieces in place while the other one traces around them.

- Color your tracing to match your pattern.

- Use a *Tile Maker Company Price Chart* to find the cost of each piece in your pattern. Then find the cost of your complete pattern. Record it.

- Design more patterns. Find the cost of each.

- Be ready to talk about how you found the cost of each pattern.

The Bigger Picture

Thinking and Sharing

Have pairs post their tracings along with the cost of each.

Use prompts such as these to promote class discussion:

- ◆ What do you notice about the prices in the price chart?

- ◆ If you knew only the price of the small triangle of each color, how could you figure out the prices of the other pieces?

- ◆ Which of the posted patterns have the same, or nearly the same, price? How are these patterns the same? How are they different?

- ◆ Using this price chart, would patterns that cover the most space always cost the most? Explain.

- ◆ Which pieces did you use most? Did you have a reason for choosing them? If so, what was your reason?

Drawing and Writing

Have pairs make the most costly tile pattern they can in the shape of a square. Have them record their pattern in color and write its cost. Then have them write a few sentences telling how they decided on their pattern.

Extending the Activity

1. Have children make and exchange outlines of their patterns. Challenge them to find different ways to fill in an outline with Tangram pieces while matching the cost of the original pattern.

2. Have children try to make the least costly pattern possible using 8 tile pieces of 3 colors.

Where's the Mathematics?

In the process of finding the total cost of a pattern, children explore the ratio of the area of the small triangle to the area of each of the other Tangram pieces. They also have an opportunity to see how multiplication and addition are related operations.

As children set out to make their 12-piece tile patterns, some may immediately set a secondary task for themselves, such as making a symmetrical shape, or making the most costly pattern possible.

A variety of strategies may be used to determine the cost of a pattern. Some children may make a list of the prices of the individual pieces and then add. Some may keep a running total. Others may make a sketch and write prices on the sketch. Still others may group like pieces or like prices and use multiplication to find a total cost for each category of tile.

As children work, they may notice that the price of each larger Tangram piece is a multiple of the price of the small triangle. Some children may choose to figure out the number of small triangles that would cover a larger piece and then multiply by the price of the small triangle of that color. This strategy shows an understanding of the area relationship among Tangram pieces. The dotted lines drawn on the green and red pattern below show how a pair would divide the pieces into numbers of small triangles in order to compute the cost of the pattern.

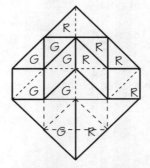

Green: 12 small triangles worth 4¢ each = 48¢

Red: 12 small triangles worth 3¢ each = 36¢

Total cost = 84¢

On the next page are a few of the many different tile patterns that children might make along with the cost of each.

3. Challenge children to use their twelve Tangram pieces to make a tile pattern that would cost exactly $1.00.

4. Have children extend the price chart by adding a fourth color of Tangrams, yellow. Have them choose a price for the small yellow triangle, then complete the price chart. They should design several four-color tile patterns, and compute the cost of each.

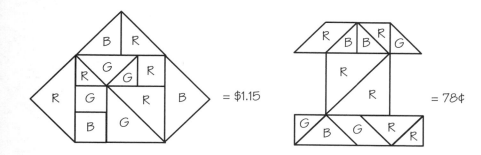 = $1.15

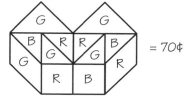

As children attempt to make the least costly pattern using eight Tangram pieces, they may notice that the red pieces have lower prices than their blue or green counterparts. Some children may attempt to use as many red pieces as possible. Others may realize that building a pattern with a small area is the best way to build the least costly pattern. The least costly 8-tile pattern will include: six small triangles, two each of blue, red, and green, and two six-cent red pieces. One possible 8-tile pattern follows.

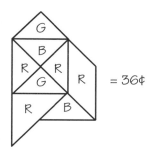 = 36¢

To make a pattern that would cost $1.00, children may begin building randomly and then add pieces as necessary to reach $1.00. Some children may figure out exactly which pieces are needed to reach $1.00 before they begin to build.

TRIANGLE MANIA

- Spatial visualization
- Non-standard measurement
- Area
- Properties of triangles

Getting Ready

What You'll Need

Tangrams, 1 set per pair

Small Tangram Triangles, 16 per pair, page 93

Overhead Tangram pieces (optional)

Overview

Children build as many different triangles as they can from one set of Tangram pieces. In this activity, children have the opportunity to:

- ◆ create and compare triangles of different sizes
- ◆ use spatial reasoning
- ◆ develop an understanding of transformational geometry
- ◆ learn about similarity

The Activity

You may want to show children how to measure the area of the squares with the small paper Tangram triangles.

Introducing

- ◆ Ask children to make squares using two or three pieces from one Tangram set.
- ◆ Confirm that there are three possibilities.
- ◆ Have children discuss how the squares are different and how they are the same.

On Their Own

How many different-size triangles can you make with a Tangram set?

- Work with a partner. Make a triangle with 2 or more Tangram pieces.

- Find the area of your triangle. Use the small Tangram triangle to measure.

- Record your triangle and its area. Keep track of the pieces you used so that you will be able to build the triangle again.

- Continue to make and record triangles until you think you have found all the possible triangles. Then, cut out each triangle.

- Be prepared to discuss how your triangles are alike and how they are different.

The Bigger Picture

Thinking and Sharing

Invite volunteers, one at a time, to post or draw a solution on the chalkboard. Continue until all of the children's solutions have been recorded and everyone agrees that there are no duplicates. Consider shapes with the same area to be different only if they are made with different pieces or if the pieces are arranged differently.

Use prompts such as these to promote class discussion:

- What do you notice about the posted shapes?

- How many different areas are displayed? Have all the possible areas been found? Explain.

- How many different triangles of each size did we find?

- How do the triangles with the same area differ?

- How did you go about making new triangles?

- Which pieces did you use most often? Which pieces were the most difficult to use?

- How are the triangles alike? How are they different?

Extending the Activity

1. Have children find the perimeter of each of the triangles they made.

2. Have children repeat this activity, this time using two sets of Tangrams.

3. Have children repeat the activity, making squares, rectangles, or parallelograms instead of triangles.

Where's the Mathematics?

Of the different-sized triangles that can be made from two or more pieces from one set of Tangram pieces, the smallest has an area of two and the largest has an area of 16. The examples below are not drawn in proportion and so the labels S, M, and L are used to label the small, medium, and large triangles.

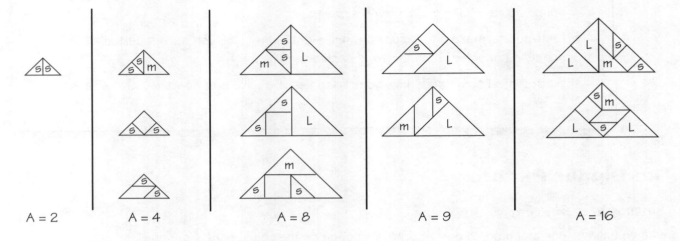

With the exception of the smallest triangle, there is more than one way to make each of the other triangles.

Every triangle made from the Tangram pieces is an isosceles triangle; that is, every triangle has two sides of the same length. Every triangle is a right triangle because the two equal sides are perpendicular to each other, and thus form a right angle. Since all the triangles are right and isosceles, they are similar to each other. To children, this means the triangles look exactly alike but are of different sizes.

In mathematical terms, the corresponding angles of similar triangles contain the same number of degrees and the corresponding sides are in the same proportion. To illustrate, compare triangle ABC to triangle DEF. When positioned as shown, ∠A corresponds to ∠D, ∠B to ∠E, and ∠C to ∠F.

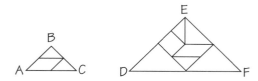

Putting one triangle on top of the other proves the corresponding angles are congruent. The sides can be matched and compared in the same way. Side $\overline{DE}$ is twice as long as its corresponding side, $\overline{AB}$, side $\overline{EF}$ is twice as long as side $\overline{BC}$, and $\overline{DF}$ is twice as long as $\overline{AC}$. All the sides are in the same ratio: 1 to 2 (1:2) or 1/2, that is, the sides are in the same proportion. Not all triangles, however, are in the ratio of 1 to 2. The ratio of the sides of any posted triangle with an area of 9 compared to the sides of any triangle with an area of 16 is 3 to 4.

Children may also notice that the triangles are symmetrical. Each can be folded along a line of symmetry that goes from the right angle to the midpoint of the opposite side. What may surprise some children, however, is that triangles with the same area can be made from different numbers of Tangram pieces. As children learn about equivalence—for example, two small triangles equals a square—this resolves itself.

In addition to finding area and examining similarities and differences among the triangles, children improve their spatial visualization as they flip, rotate, and perform other transformations in their attempt to find new triangles.

TWENTY QUESTIONS

- • Spatial visualization
- • Properties of polygons
- • Language of mathematics

Getting Ready

What You'll Need

Tangrams, 2 sets of 1color per group

Tangram paper, page 109

Overhead Tangram pieces and/or
Tangram paper transparency (optional)

Overview

In this game for two to four players, children take turns making secret shapes from Tangram pieces and asking questions in order to discover the shapes made by others. In this activity, children have the opportunity to:

- ◆ identify attributes of Tangram shapes
- ◆ use mathematical language to describe Tangram shapes
- ◆ develop listening and problem-solving skills

The Activity

Before playing the game, have the class decide whether the sides of the Tangram pieces should match. Point out that the shapes will be harder to copy if the sides do not line up exactly.

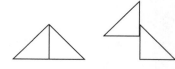

Easier   Harder

Introducing

- ◆ Model the game *Twenty Questions*. Tell children that you are thinking of a classroom object and that they may ask up to twenty yes/no questions in order to guess your object.
- ◆ Have a volunteer come to the board to keep a tally of the number of questions asked.
- ◆ After children guess your object, lead a discussion about which questions were most helpful and which did not help at all.
- ◆ Have the class play the game a few more times, calling on different volunteers to think of an object.
- ◆ Tell children that they will now play the game *Twenty Questions* and ask questions about Tangram shapes.

On Their Own

Play *Twenty Questions!*

Here are the rules:

1. This is a game for 2 to 4 players. The object of the game is to guess the Shape Designer's secret shape. Players decide who will be the first Shape Designer.

2. The Shape Designer secretly chooses 3 pieces from 2 Tangram sets and uses them to make a secret shape.

3. The other players are the Guessers. They take turns asking yes/no questions about the shape.

4. One player keeps track of how many questions are asked.

5. The Guessers use the answers to try to make a Tangram shape that looks like the Shape Designer's.

6. The game ends when either of these events occurs:

   ◆ the Guessers match the secret shape; or else

   ◆ 20 questions have been asked.

• Play several games of *Twenty Questions*. Take turns being the Shape Designer. With each new game, see if you can guess the shape in fewer questions.

• Be ready to talk about good questions and bad questions.

The Bigger Picture

Thinking and Sharing

Invite children to talk about their games and describe some of the thinking they did.

Use prompts like these to promote class discussion:

◆ What did you notice about the shapes that were made after just one or two questions were asked? What do you notice about the shapes that could not be made even after twenty questions?

◆ As the Shape Designer, when you built your shape, did you do anything to make your shape hard to guess? Did you do anything to make it easy to guess?

◆ Which shapes were the most difficult to match? Which were the easiest?

◆ When it was your turn to ask a question, how did you decide what question to ask?

◆ Which questions were most helpful in matching the shape? Which questions were least helpful?

Writing

Have groups make secret shapes from three or more Tangram pieces. Then have them a make a list of clues about their shapes that could be used by another group to copy their shape without seeing it. Have groups exchange lists and follow the clues trying to copy one another's shapes

Teacher Talk

Where's the Mathematics?

As children play this guessing game, they may begin to understand the importance of phrasing questions carefully. Their mathematical vocabulary may become more varied and precise.

Children may need to be shown how to keep a tally of the questions as they are being asked.

||| |||| |||| ||||

3 questions   5 questions   9 questions

|||| |||| |||| ||||

20 questions

Once they understand how each group of five questions is recorded, most children enjoy identifying the numbers tallied by counting by fives, and then counting on.

Children may use their first few questions to figure out which pieces make up the Shape Designer's shape. Once they know the three Tangram pieces used, they may begin to ask questions about the placement of the pieces. For example, they may ask questions such as "Does the small triangle touch the large triangle?" or "Is the square above the parallelogram?" Using this strategy, they may have difficulty copying the shape even with twenty questions.

As children continue to play the game, they may begin to notice that some questions yield more information than others. For example, in these sample questions, notice how Question B gives children more information to act upon than Question A.

    Question A: *Is the shape a square?*

If the answer is *yes*, children try to make a square from their Tangram pieces. If the answer is *no*, children have little new information to help them copy the shape.

Extending the Activity

Have children play *Twenty Questions* again, this time either increasing the number of Tangram pieces the Shape Designer uses or allowing the Shape Designer to work with two Tangram sets of different colors.

Question B: *Does the shape have four sides?*

If the answer is *yes*, children may try to make a four-sided figure, including a square, from their Tangram pieces. If the answer is *no*, children may focus on making shapes with three or five or more sides.

Each time children play the game, they are likely to improve in their ability to ask good questions. Consider the following scenario that might ensue during the third or fourth game:

Suppose the Shape Designer makes this shape:

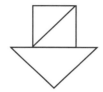

Children may ask the following questions:

Question: *Are all the pieces triangles?*

Answer: *Yes.* (This eliminates the use of the square and the parallelogram.)

Question: *Are any two of the triangles the same size?*

Answer: *Yes.* (Either the shape has two small or two large triangles.)

Question: *Are the two same-size triangles large?*

Answer: *No.* (This makes it clear that the three pieces that make up the shape are the two small triangles and either one medium or one large triangle.)

When children begin putting their pieces together to copy the shape, they may ask questions about the long and short sides of the triangles. They may ask whether the shape has any square corners, or right angles, or whether two of the pieces form a regular polygon, such as a larger triangle or a square. These kinds of questions may increase children's understanding of deduction and the use of the process of elimination in making decisions.

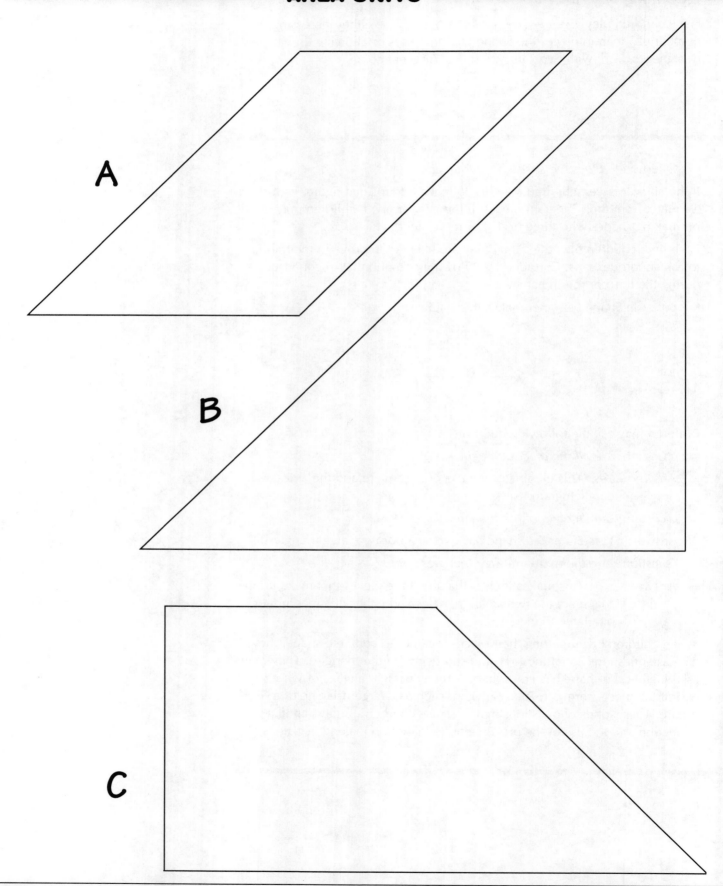

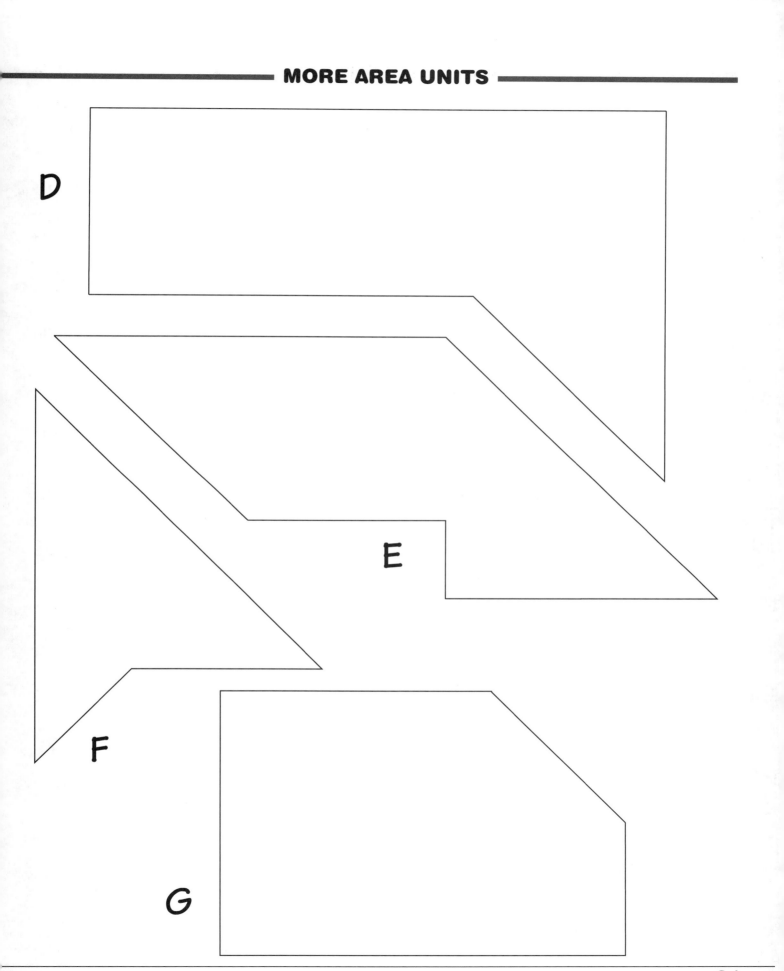

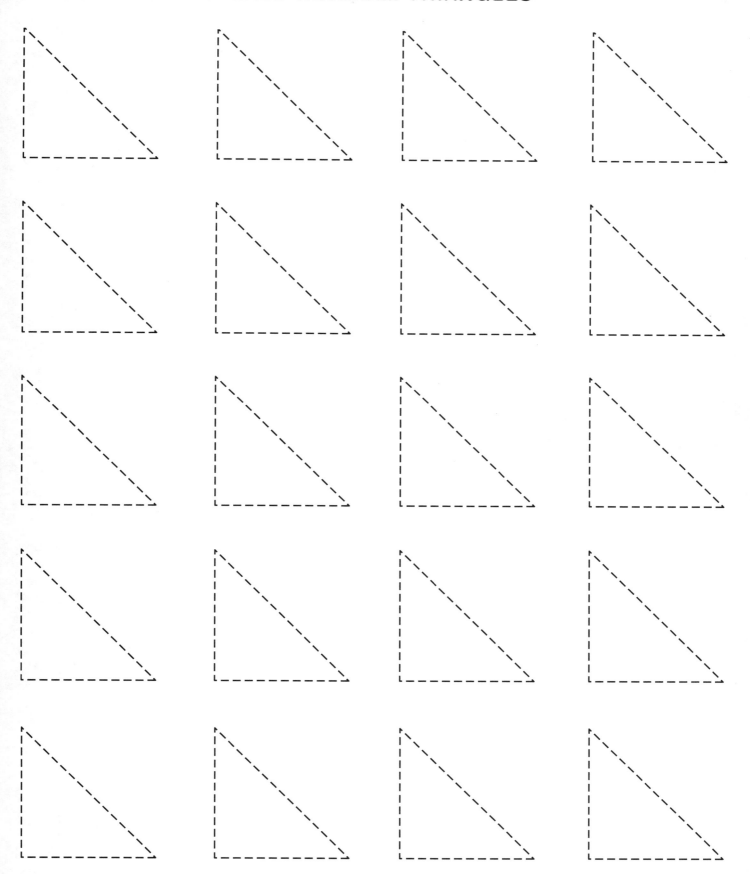

The Tangram Ruler is marked in centimeters and half centimeters.

SLIDE	FLIP	TURN
SLIDE	FLIP	TURN
SLIDE	FLIP	TURN
SLIDE	FLIP	TURN

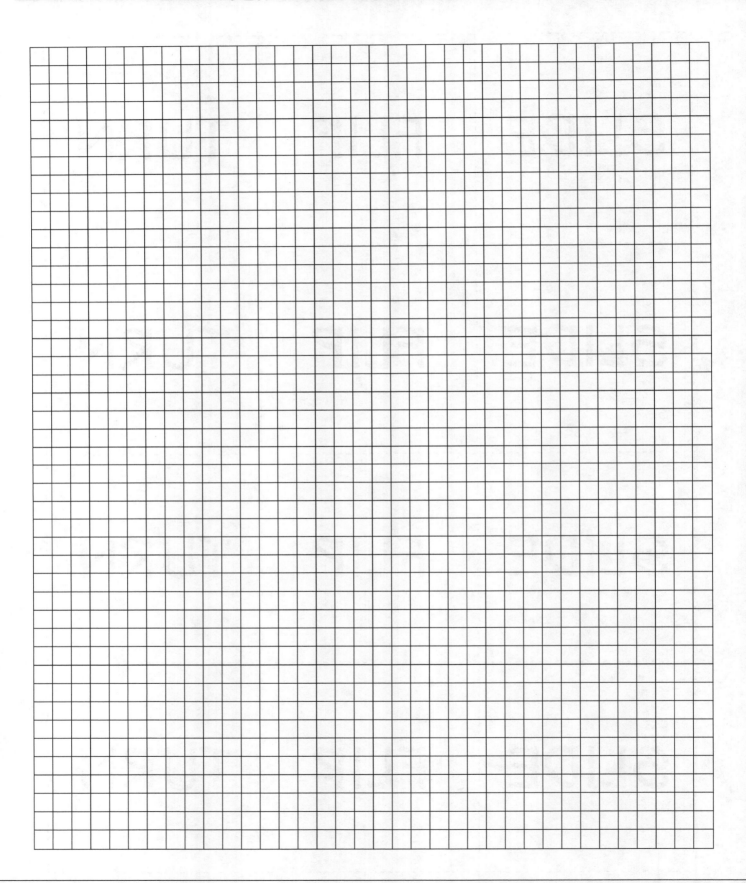

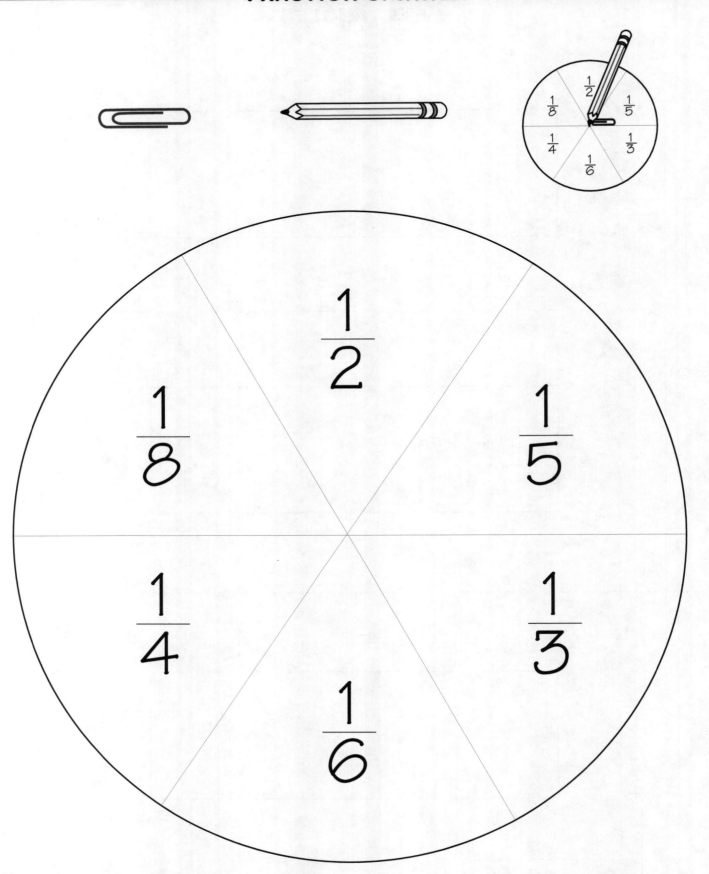

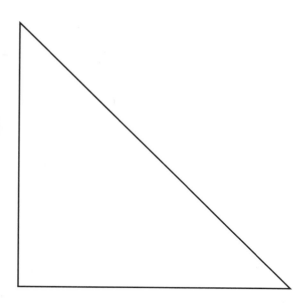

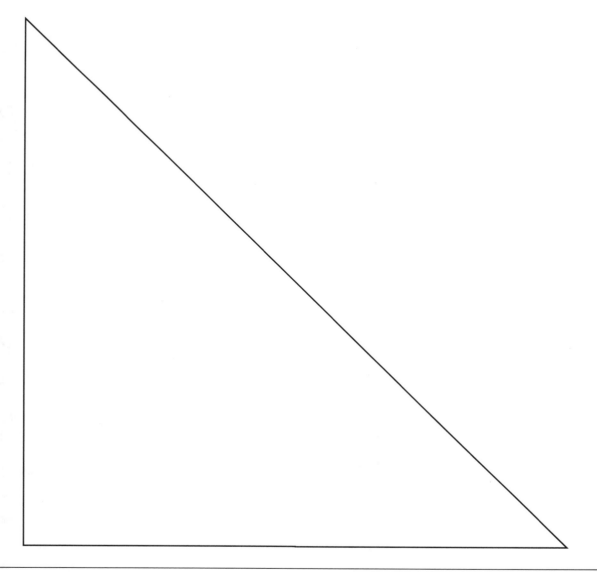

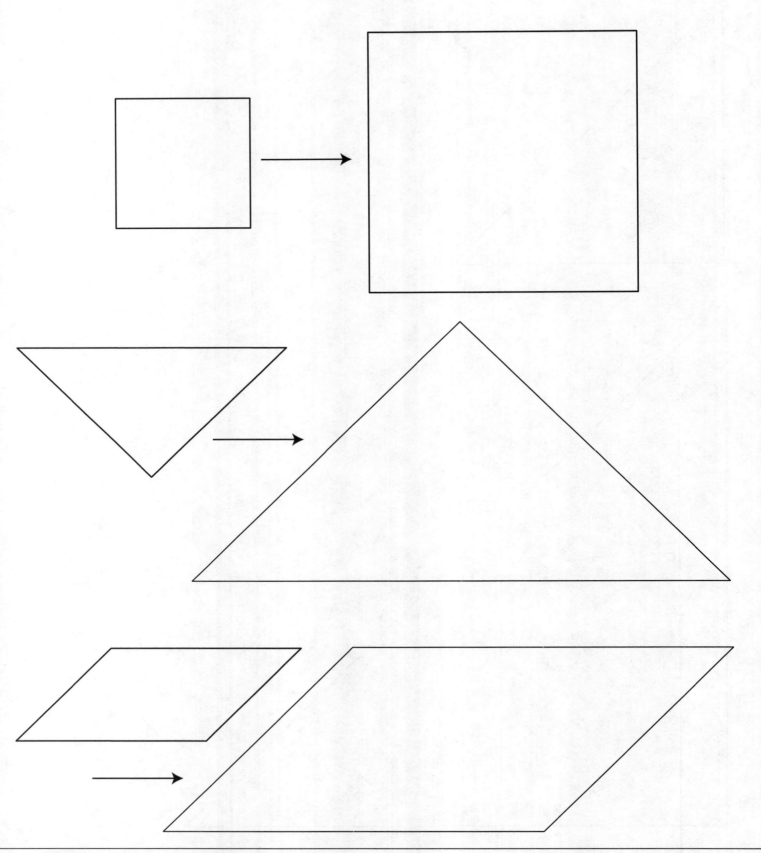

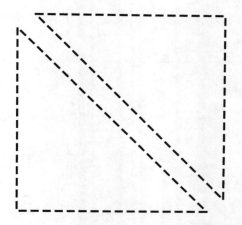
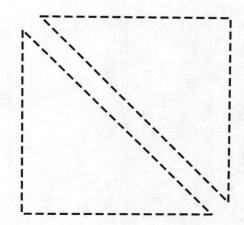

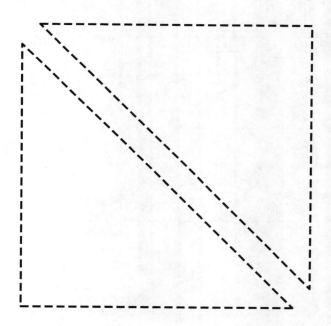
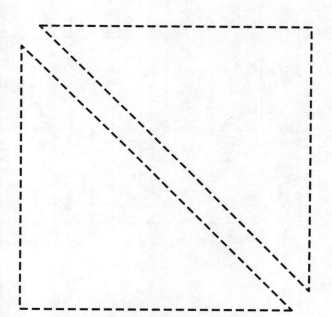

ONE CHANGE AT A TIME CARDS

TRIANGLE 3 sides	PARALLELOGRAM 4 sides opposite sides parallel no right angles
SQUARE 4 congruent sides 4 right angles	QUADRILATERAL WITH NO PARALLEL SIDES 4 sides
RECTANGLE 4 sides, not all congruent 4 right angles	CONVEX PENTAGON 5 sides no indents
TRAPEZOID 4 sides 2 parallel sides	CONCAVE PENTAGON 5 sides indents

ONE CHANGE AT A TIME CARDS

HEXAGON 6 sides	OCTAGON 8 sides
HEXAGON WITH LINE SYMMETRY 6 sides	DECAGON 10 sides
HEXAGON WITH NO LINE SYMMETRY 6 sides	POLYGON WITH 3 RIGHT ANGLES
HEPTAGON 7 sides	POLYGON WITH NO RIGHT ANGLES

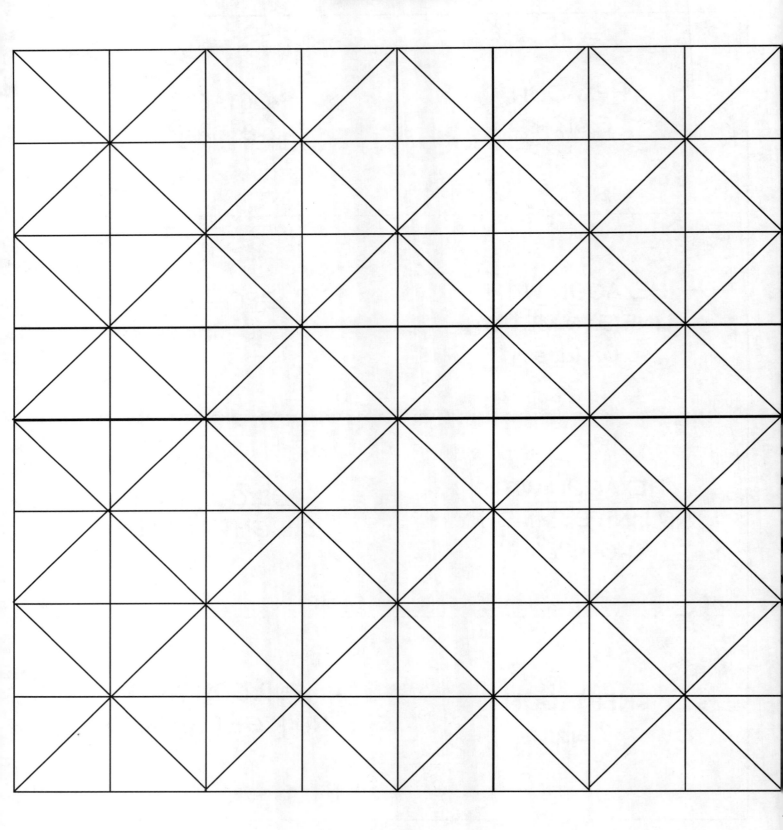

SMALL TRIANGLE SPINNER

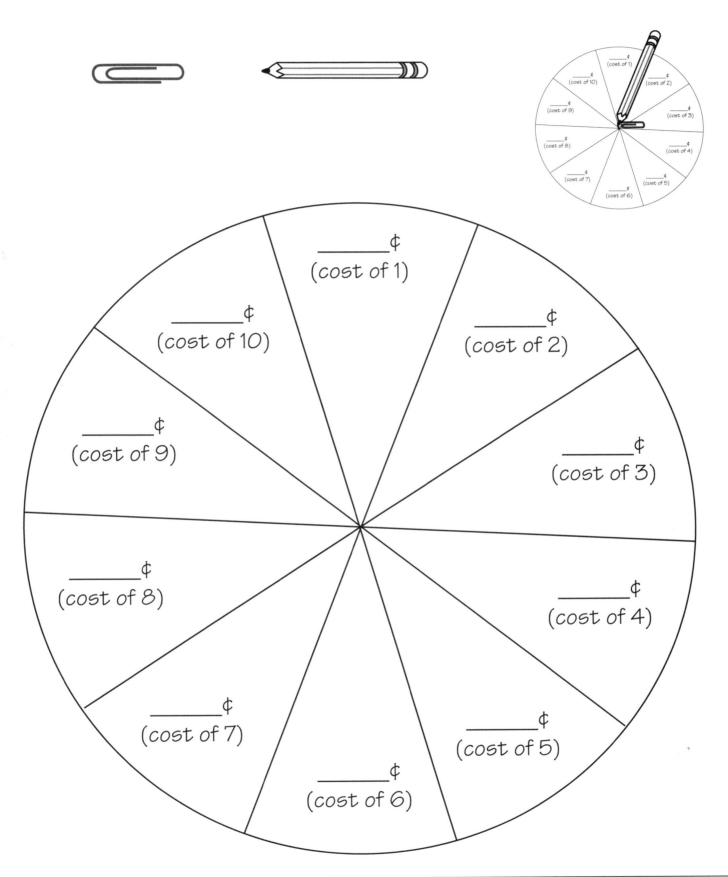

blue	5¢	10¢	20¢	10¢	10¢
red	3¢	6¢	12¢	6¢	6¢
green	4¢	8¢	16¢	8¢	8¢

1-CENTIMETER GRID PAPER